7 CORE WOUNDS
GROWTH AND HOW

HEAL

YOUR SOUL

HEAL YOUR BUSINESS

LATARA VENISE
JOLANDA ROGERS

FOREWORD BY: JANICE ANDERSON

Copyright © 2021 Heal Your Business Academy
Title: Heal Your Soul Heal Your Business
Subtitle: 7 Core Wounds Blocking Your Business Growth and How to Break Through Them
ISBN: 978-1-952327-73-5
Library of Congress Control Number: 2021951049

Printed in the United States of America
T.A.L.K. Publishing, LLC
talkconsulting.net

Heal Your Business Academy
healyourbusiness.academy

HEAL YOUR SOUL HEAL YOUR BUSINESS
Where Soul Healing and Business Transformation Happen

This work is dedicated to those longing to heal their soul and heal their business.

A.J., Dinetra, Emerald, Felicia, Jennifer, Lashondra, Nancy, Sandra, Sonia, Stacey, and Stephen, thank you for sharing your heart and taking the journey with us.

JoLanda & LaTara

To my sons, Alexander "AJ" and Brehane. Thank you for being two of my biggest fans and my partners in healing. I am who I am because of who you both are in my life. I love you both all the way up to heaven.

— LaTara Venise

Bridgette, I admire your brilliance, and humor. You are a beautiful reflection of your mom; thank you for sharing her with me.

JVN, no words but thank you, and I know you understand the sentiments of my heart.

Kim, we are "tribe"— you are a courageous soul on so many levels; thank you for being on the journey with me.

Mindy, you are the most authentic soul I have ever met in my life. Thank you for the safety in your friendship.

Talva, my love, thank you for doing life with me—. I do what I do **because** of you. TaLanda, Ajaa, Kaedance, and TJ—. I do what I do **for** you. You are my strength to heal deeper. Heal Your Soul Heal Your Business would not even be a thing without you.

– JoLanda

CONTENTS

FOREWORD

*H*eal Your Soul, Heal Your Business* may be one of the most important business books you will ever read. JoLanda and LaTara have joined forces with the agenda of heaven to expose and eradicate common but often overlooked barriers to sustained business success. These roadblocks cripple many faith-filled believers—but not for long.

JoLanda and LaTara are women of great faith whose personal journeys through life and business have been marked by their relentless pursuit of God's best. They are more than mere researchers of this work. Through tears and prayers, though trained professionals themselves, these women have partnered with God and skilled specialists to discover the work, do the work, and employ personal habits to maintain the work required to live and enjoy a whole and free life. The process is not easy—but every step you take toward your wholeness is worth it.

As a corporate career woman turned CEO, I have secretly endured the pain and feelings of defeat that accompany the debilitating cycles unhealed wounds create. The inner chaos and conflict with not being able to identify, let alone fix the brokenness that kept me from my next level was exhausting. I remember relentlessly searching for answers: praying, crying, researching, taking classes, obtaining certifications and degrees, buying products and programs, attending conferences and events—all to no avail. Nothing was enough.

I finally realized that the work I needed to do was less obvious, less popular, and less glamorous. Healing my wounded heart was a journey that required me—not my intellect, my hard work, my money, nor my expertise. Nope, my healing required me—the stripped naked version—more specifically, the parts I had stuffed and tucked to survive. Especially those parts. I had no idea how my hidden places of pain and shame impacted my ability to progress freely.

Today, on the other side of much work is much progress and an abundance of joy. I have peace of mind. I make profitable decisions. I serve well—because I am well. My business and my life are thriving—not because I am perfect. Girl . . . Don't get me started on my imperfections (that's another book). I simply choose to live my life in pursuit of healing, wholeness, and deep, relational intimacy with my heavenly Father.

Along my journey, I've discovered a few misconceptions among believers that often keep us stuck in cycles of not enough or just enough in business.

The belief that your faith can outperform your lack of business acumen is foolish

I have personally been the recipient of many miracles and God-alone-did-this blessings in my lifetime—too many to count. Yet, I am certain God never intended for us to live nor operate as business owners from miracle to miracle. We are expected to study and put in practice to become skilled laborers in our chosen professions. Proverbs 22:29 in the Holman Christian Standard Bible reads:

Do you see a man skilled in his work?
He will stand in the presence of kings.
He will not stand in the presence of unknown men.

The King James translation of that same verse uses diligent to describe skilled; the Hebrew word translates to "quick, prompt, ready and skillful" (Strong, 2009). When it comes to our work, Scripture reveals we are rewarded for our capability, not merely our availability. For further study, consider these passages that outline the reward of the diligent (a.k.a. skillful): Proverbs 10:4, Proverbs 12:27, Proverbs 13: 5, and Proverbs 21:5. To see this concept modeled in Scripture, note the type of people chosen to construct the tabernacle as found in Exodus 31:6, 35:10, and 36:1. Our faith does not exempt us from faithfulness—do what's required to be considered a master of your craft.

The belief that hard work and "head work" cancel the need for "heart work."

As a natural-born strategist with a love for learning, my default way of handling obstacles is to research the solution, create a plan, and work my plan. I once believed everything could be resolved with a plan and consistent action. This belief was supported by my constant enrollment in school, workshops, or certifications in my field of interest. Whenever I ran into a roadblock, I took a class or purchased a program. Don't get me wrong; this willingness to learn has served me well—I am a sharp, well-educated, capable woman.

In my area of expertise, I am definitely among the top 10 percent of learners and doers.

My search for solutions didn't stop there—I learned early in this journey that if I wanted to see the success of my efforts, I must couple my skills training with mindset work. Neuroscience has finally caught up with the revelation of Scripture, providing substantial evidence that we humans have the ability to change the physical structure of our brains and subsequently our lives with our thoughts. Wow! Paul states it this way: "And be not conformed to this world: but be ye transformed by the renewing of your mind" (Romans 12:2 KJV). As we intentionally take control of our thought life, we can positively shift our human experience in spite of our circumstances.

Regardless of what I face today, I am certain I have the skillset, the mindset, and the stamina to find a way or make a way. Yet, at various points in my life and career, neither my quality of life, influence in my industry, nor my bank account reflected my impeccable work ethic, positive mindset, nor diligent studies. At times, I had nothing or very little at best to show for my hard work. This often caused me to second-guess my competency and my credibility. Over time, I began to shrink back. There were even seasons of life where instead of dreaming, I was settling. For years I didn't understand what was missing. I prayed and cried many nights—God, what did I do wrong? Show me the error of my ways. And then I prayed Psalm 139:23–24 (KJV): "Search me, O God, and know my heart: try me, and know my thoughts: And see if there be any wicked way in me, and lead me in the way everlasting." When studying this passage, I learned that the psalmist was asking God to examine him thoroughly. His desperation for help was such that he wanted the almighty God to check him out and give it to him straight. The Hebrew definition for the words used in this passage means the following:

- heart - the seat of the senses, affections, and emotions of mind; the soul
- thoughts - secrets
- wicked – pain, hurtful

The psalmist was essentially asking, As you perform a divine x-ray on me, please let me know the secrets I am holding on to that are hurting me or causing me pain. Reveal to me that which stands between me and your promises. To that prayer, God replied to me in the most loving and compassionate manner possible, "Your broken heart." To neglect your heart work is to diminish the impact of your hard work. Do the heart work.

The belief that heart work is a once-and-done matter is delusional.

I have been described as a make-it-happen woman—the kind of woman you want on your team, in your circle, and a part of your life. With this title has come the expectation (self-imposed, might I add) that once the work is done—I'm done. In times past (pre–healing and wholeness), any time I have had to rework a task, I felt inadequate. I felt like I had failed. As I reflect on those times and how irrational my expectations were of myself, I think, Man that had to be tough. I bet I was tired inside. What an injustice this line of reasoning projects on our hearts. Mistakes, missteps, and errors in judgment are not an indication of failure or inadequacy. Not always. It is important in life and in business that you remain curious. Some things require time to resolve. Some obstacles will require continual effort to overcome. Some hurts need consistent work and multiple revisits to heal and fully recover—practice compassion. Embrace self-compassion as a way of life. I have—and I am grateful for it.

As a strategist by profession, I know a reliable strategy is a tested strategy. Testing is part of the process. One way I practice self-compassion in my business is by informing all prospective agency clients of our team's approach to obtaining their desired outcomes: (1) we test, (2) we track, (3) we tweak, and (4) we try again. Of course, I don't guarantee results. But, I guarantee we will execute based on proven systems with skill and strategy, using best practices together with ethically and spiritually sound approaches.

It took years for me to get to this place of freedom. I had to first understand and accept that though I was moving forward, my heart was in desperate need of attention. My heart had been gravely mishandled—some wounds were apparent, most were not; each of them impacted my life and my business. Yet, today I can reflect and celebrate how far I've come. I can see and savor the fruit of my heart work. My marriage is still fun even though there are hard moments; motherhood is exciting and challenging, yet it does not define me, and my business is not the source of my legitimacy. I am significant beyond these roles, not because of them.

I pray as you embark upon your healing journey that you remember this—

On the other side of heart work awaits:

- an increased capacity to receive and give unconditional love,
- an unshakable joy,
- peace beyond your wildest dreams,

- an abundance of a divine portion,
- and more heart work.

Embrace your journey, make time to slow down and savor the moment, and remember to celebrate your progress—every moment matters!

Janice L. Anderson
Daughter of the King
Wife of Maurice L. Anderson
Mother of Jasmine, Jada, and Journey
Founder and CEO, Moruwa Consulting
Founder, Significant Life

PREFACE

A Quick Recap of What This Book Is and What This Book Is Not

Before you move forward and for you to get the most out of this work, we want to be sure you understand what this book is and what this book is not.

What this book is:

- This book is a brief introduction to a selection of soul wounds and how they may manifest in your business and your life.
- This book is a work that was prayerfully considered and specifically written with you in mind.
- This book is an invitation to a deeper healing journey that will enrich your mind, body, and soul.
- This book comprises individuals committed to engaging in business from a healed posture in which they facilitate soul care and live a life dedicated to a personal soul healing journey.
- This book is a resource that you can use to explore, identify, and acknowledge where there may be wounds in your soul blocking your business growth.

What this book is not:

- This book is not the only resource and tool you'll need to heal your soul and heal your business.
- This book is not intended to be the start and stop of your healing journey. It is a companion for the road forward.
- This book is not a work to read critically or quickly. Pause at each section and observe what is stirred up or moving inside of you.
- This book is not just another book on how to grow your business and improve your results. We intend for you to experience soul transformation.
- This book is not where you stop; once you are done, join us at healyourbusiness.academy, where you can experience healing available for your soul and your business.

INTRODUCTION

Soul wounds are those injuries in our lives that go so deep that our very identities are changed. We carry these invisible scars into our world of work, creating holes in the fabric of our business. Wounded in life, we are called into business. As faith-filled business leaders, God calls us into the journey of healing our souls. This journey is a lifetime commitment without a distinct arrival point. Frustrating, right? Not completely. When we can learn to love the journey, we can wait with grace for the destination.

Heal Your Soul – Heal Your Business will help you identify core soul wounds and explain what they are, how they manifest in your work world, and how to walk the healing path. As you embrace this work, please know this is not a bashing party for caregivers you love or a pity symposium to have your deepest wounds overtake you. It is an intentional invitation to acknowledge ways you've been wounded throughout your life and how the impacts of these wounds could be wreaking havoc in your business and, likely, your personal life.

Let's agree together that everyone has wounds; no one is exempt. Does that make us eternally doomed? No, it creates an awareness that if we have not addressed how we've been wounded, the impact may still be alive and well inside us. Let's also agree that while every person has wounds, each person has also wounded someone else. Does that make us eternally damned? No, it makes us human, living life with other humans.

As we approach and unpack the seven wounds selected for this work, we are not naive to the reality that some wounds were intentional, and they were not the result of anything you did or did not do. Acknowledging this is important because it dishonors the experience of hearts that have been broken by fallen humanity if we do not. Wounds can damage us on a cellular level; there are countless studies on the neurobiology of how we respond to life events and how traumatic events become locked inside of our bodies. We know that just as trauma and wounds can manifest in the body, they can manifest in your business.

With this knowledge, we don't expect nor proclaim to have the answer. However, we know who holds the answers and the healing. As faith-filled business leaders, our reliance on true soul healing is entirely upon God. While this book will provide insight and even direction on how to begin and continue a healing journey, it is through God and Him alone that this healing is possible. We wrote this book from inside our healing journeys and experiences. We've felt the pain of the process; we know the freedom that awaits and the business success that follows!

Although we've selected seven core wounds that we've seen as primary assailants for an emerging or thriving business owner— mother wounds, father wounds, wounds of trust, wounds of abuse, wounds of loss, wounds of unresolved issues, and wounds of rejection—we are aware there are more that can be added to this list. As we explore the wounds, we will unpack our working definition of each wound, how they manifest in business, provide a soul in business with biblical balm for addressing the wound, and offer context for a healing journey of each wound.

We believe a journey is experienced best when walked alongside another person. To model this, we've included testimonies from business owners in various service-based industries and those who serve in leadership roles in their corporate careers. Often when we are wounded in community, community is also what brings deep healing to our lives. The contributing authors aren't just sharing something they heard or about a course they attended. Each author is pouring from the heart of their respective experiences and how they've seen their businesses and their lives heal by the decision and commitment to healing their soul.

We want you to know we created this work with you in mind. Let's heal your soul and heal your business, together.

MOTHER WOUNDS

Mother is our first home and introduction to life as we initially know it. It doesn't matter how old you are, what you've accomplished, or where you've gone; your mother's influence marks your life until the day you die. She is, in fact, your very first influencer. Yes, you may have a fantastic coach who has helped you establish the foundation of your business, but your mother was your very first coach. The home she provided in her womb wired within your developing body what to expect from the world around you. When we talk about the mother wound as one of the seven core soul wounds that can create havoc in our business, we are talking about the severe impact of a mother's neglect, absence, abuse, or lack of love that makes a hole in our soul and a hole in our business.

Remember, our mother is home for us while we are in the womb. She is our source of life, nourishment, protection, and love when we are born. It is the mother who nurses us, feeds us, changes us, cuddles us, and looks into our face with love and attachment. She comforts us when we cry—her very body is attuned to our cry with the let-down nursing response. This means when a mother nurses a baby and the baby cries, her body prepares to respond by producing milk as comfort. Her body was created to meet every need of that child. In this one example, the economic, social, and educational playing field becomes leveled in our mothering experience. We can see how mothers have a God-given ability within their own body to take care of the needs of a distressed child.

She cleans us when we are soiled, covers us when we are cold. She tells us that we smell wonderful, and she knows exactly how we like to be held and what helps us feel safe and peaceful. We find rest in the crook of her neck or against the softness of her breast. Our mother gives us a sense of being and belonging. We trust that we are loved and cared for in our utterly vulnerable infancy.

Readers of this description will likely have multiple reactions based on their maternal experience and bonding. Here is an invitation to a personal moment: Notice what you feel in your body. Notice how your heart responds to the discussion of the critical provisions a mother offers.

- Is there a lump in your throat or tension in your face, being aware of the sense of belonging and safety a mother offers?
- Is your stomach mildly unsettled at the wonder of your first home?
- Do you feel nothing at all?
- Did you smile, reminiscing on the secure attachment with your mother?
- Did you wonder about the attachment of your children to you?

Pay attention, and notice.

Unpacking the Mother Wound

A mother wound happens when this bond is broken, or a child is unable to develop a secure attachment to the mother. Perhaps we didn't bond with our mother because she was too ill or died.

Maybe we were the ones sick and had to be hospitalized for a long time. Perhaps she already had children and couldn't give time and attention to us as she expended all her energy on her large family. Maybe she was a single parent and needed to work, and we experienced a variety of different caregivers. Maybe her parenting of us was broken by her inadequacy and mother wound or by addiction or mental illness. Whatever may have caused it, we experience our mother wound as a profound sense of emptiness and rejection. Other feelings include being unlovable, not worth caring for, and having low self-esteem. The mother wound profoundly impacts us is in our ability to connect meaningfully with others.

The Mother Wound in Business

Over the years, the mother wound may manifest in different ways that impact our business life and keep us from the success we desire. We may struggle with codependency, becoming overly dependent on other women for their approval, support, and nurture. Codependent relationships may camouflage themselves as really good business buddies. One way to know when the boundaries have been blurred is each individual's responses when separation is necessary or when a disagreement happens. The business owner wounded by the mother will question their worthiness, work hard to mend the relationship even if it is unhealthy, create proximity-seeking opportunities to be with the other individual, and more.

Depending on the personality, temperament, and natural wiring, a mother-wounded business owner may also find themselves pushing other women away, protecting themselves through independence and self-reliance. We will have trouble working with women as our supervisors but also as our supervisees.

We may have trouble acknowledging our nurturing side—or alternatively, smother others with our misplaced mothering! Unconsciously, we might be misogynists, feeling a kind of contempt and prejudice against women even as we apparently advocate for them. We may say things like I prefer to work with men over women or I don't do women or women are too emotional, too complicated, too (fill in the blank).

The mother wound will cause us to struggle with self-care and fight against balance, boundaries, and healthy limits.

A Soul in Business Biblical Balm for the Mother Wound

When we are wounded, a balm brings healing. A balm offers soothing relief for wherever our ache is. We believe in the context of soul healing; there is no greater balm, no greater soothing element than the Word of God. A mother's love is a soothing balm to our developing souls; remember, a secure attachment to a mother's love will give us a sense of being.

To experience healing in the profound soul wound from the mother is transforming. It generates a healthy view of love, understanding and deepens our capacity for relational wisdom.

A Healthy View of Maternal Love
from LaTara Venise, Vision Activation Strategist

A baby's first love connection is with their mother. After being conceived, the baby lives with its mother exclusively for nine months. As a mother of two boys, I can attest to the fact that the baby feels what you feel, and they are born with those emotions intertwined into their character and personality. It is important in this instance for the mother to provide love, safety, and security even while the child is in the womb and once the child is born to continue to love the child without condition.

I noticed from the womb that my youngest son felt every emotion I had. There was a moment during a Fourth of July boat parade when it became very evident to me. I was anxious about being around a bunch of people and walking for what seemed to be forever while seven months pregnant. My mood was off, and I was ready to go home, but my husband wanted to wait until the fireworks show. That threw my anxiety into forward motion and had a direct effect on Brehane. As soon as the fireworks show started, he began to jump in my belly so hard and fast that you could make out his body. As I prayed, rubbed my belly, and calmed down, he did the same. It was definitely a moment I'll never forget and an awareness that everything my soul felt, his soul, and body experienced. The same is true for you and me as our mothers were our first home.

A Biblical Look at Healing the Mother Wound

"Above all, love each other deeply, because love covers over a multitude of sins" (1 Peter 4:8 NIV). It is unconditional love that covers a multitude of sins, and sin is anything opposite of God. When we worry, set unhealthy boundaries and expectations, and have anxiety in our lives, we are walking opposite of God. That in itself is lending itself to the sinful nature.

The mother should exhibit the love of God, and when it is lacking, the resulting wound causes the business owner to either under or over-perform. When unconditional love is balanced, it provides the support, encouragement, and motivation necessary to live out dreams and realize visions.

A mother who does not have the love of God for her child causes an imbalance in how the child perceives, receives, and achieves in life. Her love needs to align with the words Paul penned in 1 Corinthians:

> Love is patient, love is kind. It does not envy, it does not boast, it is not proud. It does not dishonor others, it is not self-seeking, it is not easily angered, it keeps no record of wrongs. Love does not delight in evil but rejoices with the truth. It always protects, always trusts, always hopes, always perseveres. (1 Corinthians 13:4–7 NIV)

This sort of love gives a child a balanced view of what it looks like to unconditionally provide what the people they come in contact with day after day need. A business owner with a balanced view of love will lead their business with the heart of the Father because of the secure attachment to the mother.

The entrepreneur must make a conscious effort to find healing from mother wounds by seeking first God's unconditional love and then his wisdom in all things in their life.

The Need for Wisdom

Mothers have wisdom that will help their children thrive. When a mother is absent from the child in the formative years, it will cause the business owner to have an unhealthy flow in life, directly affecting business.

Scripture tells us that wisdom only lacks because we don't ask for it. The messenger of this word is clear when he states that all we have to do is ask, and God will provide us with wisdom. "If any of you lacks wisdom, you should ask God, who gives generously to all without finding fault, and it will be given to you" (James 1:5 NIV).

This wisdom is key for the business owner struggling with a mother wound to be able to properly guide, support, encourage, and provide in their daily business functions.

The Journey of Healing the Mother Wound

Healing the mother wound is a lifelong journey. It is transgenerational because patterns that are not broken will be carried through our parenting and mentoring into the generations to come. You will find that your mother wound will make itself known in painful ways as you parent your children and mentor those entrusted to you. Use these painful seasons to get to know your mother wound better, grieve the losses around your mothering, and forgive your mother.

Intentionally and prayerfully seek out older female mentors and prayer warriors. Develop a support network that will walk through the years with you. Include women who are not afraid of your prickliness or independence (or sticky neediness!). Seek friends who will confront you in love and nurture you in grace. Join a professional group that includes strong female leaders and be honest about your wounds and your needs.

We can't leave this section without addressing the dysfunctional behaviors that may have served as self-soothing techniques for you. These soothing techniques are not personality or character deficiencies; they are reasonable responses to a deep wound. You will need to be intentional in addressing behaviors such as misuse of food, substances, sex, or gambling. There are good anonymous twelve-step groups that will help you navigate these and develop healthy ways of self-nurture.

Learn how to self-soothe through nature, relaxation breathing, gentle exercise, beauty, and music. Listen to your critical self-talk and be kind and tenderhearted to yourself. Spend time with people who appreciate you and help you to relax.

John Bradshaw did pioneer work on reparenting the inner child in his Homecoming: Reclaiming and championing your inner child (1990). You will also benefit from Lucia Capacchione's Recovery of your inner child (1991). Get referrals for good counselors and therapists who can help you understand your "internal family systems" and work toward healing the little and lost parts of yourself. Bless yourself with the gift of therapy to unravel codependent and enmeshed ways of relating that sabotage your soul and your business.

Appendix A provides questions to explore your relationship with maternal wounding, an invitation to go deeper, and an affirmation of alignment.

FATHER WOUNDS

The impact of a present and affirming father figure cannot be denied. While some are blessed to know this presence, many live with the truth of an absent father, unknown father, or a present but an emotionally unavailable father. We have known for a long time that fathers play a crucial role in the healthy development of their sons. We are discovering now that fathers also profoundly impact their daughters' sense of self and success in the world. Our fathers anchor our family and give it structure and continuity in an increasingly chaotic world. Our fathers build our sense of efficacy, of doing things and completing things, as they teach and train us. They create boundaries for us through limits, teaching us what to say yes to and what we say no to. They teach us about the value of work, of being on time, of a job well-done, and of how to handle money. They model leadership, servanthood, and respect for authority. They are safety for us as they protect us, defend us, and provide for our needs.

If all of what we describe is true about the presence of a father, then the impact of his absence or his wounding must be profound. The father wound is the soul hole that comes from a lack of fathering, a deficient or deformed father love. Dr. Daniel Passini, a specialist on the intersection of faith and technology, writes, "There is a trauma wound affecting more people than drugs or alcohol combined. It cuts deeper than flesh and bone and works its way to the soul. It affects both the rich and poor alike without prejudice. It is the father wound, and it leaves a wake of destruction in its path more devastating than any natural disaster" (2017). According to statistics gathered from Fathers Unite Campaign, an organization that equips men for fathering, children that grow up in fatherless homes are:

- 5 times more likely to commit suicide
- 32 times more likely to run away
- 20 times more likely to have behavioral disorders
- 14 times more likely to commit rape
- 9 times more likely to drop out of high school
- 20 times more likely to end up in prison (Passini, 2017)

We will pause for a moment and breathe in the harshness of that reality with you. When a father's absence, abuse, or unavailability is known to a child, they develop varying degrees of rootlessness, lack of structure, difficulty with boundaries, and difficulty with authority and with self-esteem. Your father may have failed you because of divorce, disease, death, incarceration, abuse, or indifference. Your father might not even know you exist. Still, as an adult, you will need to face the implications of the father wound that so injured your soul.

It is likely that if father wounds have impacted you, you are an "external locus of control" person, meaning that you lack internal structure and depend on external cues and requirements to get things done. You have trouble relating to men in intimate friendships or committed relationships. You may experience misandry, an underlying contempt for men and male achievement. Or you may try to enhance the missing masculine side of you through same-sex attachments, promiscuity, or pornography, always seeking male affection, attention, and affirmation. The impacts of this wounding are profound for both men and women. A father's love affirms and secures our identity. When his love is absent, often, so is our sense of secure identity.

Unpacking the Father Wound

A father wound happens when a father is absent, present but absent, abusive, emotionally unavailable, or fails to provide the affirmation needed to settle one's soul in their full identity. Fathers call us out and tell us who we are. They tell us our worth and provide a foundation of boundaries and structure that empowers us to hold the highest regard for ourselves at all costs.

When a father is unknown, there is desolation in the soul of a child, and there can be instability in owning their true identity and thriving to their fullest potential. The father wound is indeed a significant one, evidenced in an individual's attention-seeking behavior, affirmation deprivation, and misaligned relationships with men.

The Father Wound in Business

The father wound can derail an entire business operation. As a business owner or leader in a corporate-level position, you must have confidence in your ability to succeed. This wound, however, will be a barrier to that confidence. Even if it is masked and a false sense of confidence is displayed, the truth of the void is often felt when the business owner is alone or during pivotal business moments where you do not show up in your full greatness. Depression and disappointment usually follow experiences of the father wound on display in our business.

Your self-esteem and identity will be wobbly; you will find yourself feeling like you are always teeter-tottering between thoughts of identity security and identity insecurity. You'll struggle with procrastination and may not feel comfortable with or worthy of success. There may be trouble planning projects and bringing them through to completion, including sabotaging your work by turning things in late or not keeping your commitments. Your struggle will manifest in your relationships with other team members as you resent their accomplishments. You either resent male authority or pander to it for acceptance. Your need for attention and affirmation may put you in risky positions or just become tiresome for you and your team. Your need for structure pushes you to leadership style extremes: micromanagement or a laissez-faire style that leads to chaos. Balance in your business leadership is elusive! You may find your conflict management skills are hindered by your anger and need to control. Take a look at some additional ways the father wound shows up in business and notice if any resonate with you:

- Improper pricing structures that devalue what is being offered.
- A grind mentality that seeks to overperform.
- No boundaries in business or too many rules and regulations.
- Improper stewarding of time, money, and people.
- Information hoarding without implementation.
- Coach hopping or having too many coaches at one time.
- Following trends and not properly vetting or understanding your purpose.

A Soul in Business Biblical Balm for the Father Wound

When we are wounded, a balm brings healing. A balm offers soothing relief for wherever our ache is. We believe in the context of soul healing; there is no greater balm, no greater soothing element than the Word of God. Our fathers affirm us. They secure us in our identity and call us out to walk in purpose. A father's love is the empowering force to stand in confidence and security, owning our place here on earth.

The Power of a Father's Presence
by LaTara Venise, Vision Activation Strategist

I loved my daddy. I was what many call a true daddy's girl, and we were really close. I was the baby of the bunch, and to this day, all of my brothers and sisters will tell you I was the one that he would do anything for. When he died in 1985, it changed the trajectory of my life. Daddy had been sick a while with colon cancer. From the age of eleven until I turned sixteen, I watched him fight a battle that he finally lost. It was devastating to my soul. I did not realize it then, but I do now. My father did not intentionally mean to, but he left me with a father wound that festered for years.

When daddy died, it started a downward spiral for me where I was always looking for love in all the wrong places. My identity became distorted because my daddy was not available at the pivotal ages that a girl needed her father. Even when he was alive, once cancer started to take over his body my identity was in question because I was just starting to come into being a young lady who would one day become a woman. I had to navigate life without my father, and that was not easy.

Father wounds, like mother wounds, stem from a biological parent or primary caregiver being absent in mind, body, or soul. Each aspect of a parent is important for the child as they grow up. Without the proper guidance, protection, and love from a father, a child who becomes an entrepreneur will likely have deep-seated esteem issues and struggle with how they identify in the marketplace.

A Biblical Look at Healing the Father Wound

> God spoke: "Let us make human beings in our image, make them, reflecting our nature so they can be responsible for the fish in the sea, the birds in the air, the cattle, and, yes, Earth itself, and every animal that moves on the face of Earth."

> God created human beings; he created them godlike, reflecting God's nature. He created them male and female. God blessed them: "Prosper! Reproduce! Fill Earth! Take charge! Be responsible for fish in the sea and birds in the air, for every living thing that moves on the face of Earth." (Genesis 1:27–28 MSG)

When God created human beings, he did so with purpose, and with that purpose came the identity of who man would be. Human beings were created in the image of God with everything they needed to move in the blessings that came with the identity. In a similar way, children are identified by who their father is, what he does, and how he does it. When a father is absent from the picture or he and the mother never married, society labels the child without a father as illegitimate. The child, to the world, is somehow unwanted or not desired, simply because the father is absent. The child often struggles to discover their identity because of how the world sees them.

"Then the Lord God formed a man from the dust of the ground and breathed into his nostrils the breath of life, and the man became a living being" (Genesis 2:7 NIV).

God gave man life; so does the earthly father. When a man and woman create a child, it is the father who gives sperm to the woman so that her egg can produce a child. It is how life is formed. Once that child is conceived, it has been given an identity. It then becomes the duty of the earthly father to help that child develop purpose within that identity. If the father is absent—mentally, physically, or emotionally—then the child's identity often becomes distorted. So then, in business, that misidentified person shows up often seeking approval, searching for love in the wrong places, without proper structure, and not understanding their worth.

The goal for the business owner struggling with these wounds is to work at properly aligning their identity with who God says they are and what he breathed into them. Life, purpose, and his identity.

The Journey of Healing the Father Wound

Will the real you, please stand up? No, not that one, the other one. No, not that one either, the other one. We're sure you can understand where this is going and where it continues to go. It is the search for identity and who you truly are. This hole in your soul is so familiar that you might overlook it or have made friends with it. The father wound can begin to feel like a natural part of life or cause you to adapt a this-is-just-the-way-I-am type of attitude. So many of us function as best we can with vague father-longings, not realizing the prominent role this wound plays in our lives and business.

HEAL YOUR SOUL - HEAL YOUR BUSINESS

The healing journey takes time. A father is not easily replaced, even when stepfathers and other male figures stand in the gap; there is something to be said about the biological connection between a father and child. Without this, the deep identity work is hard and costly. Terry Wardle, author of Wounded: How to find wholeness and inner healing in Christ and founder and president of Healing Care Ministries (https://www.healingcare.org/), offers a program of inner healing and transformation. While many other wounds may surface and are addressed during this process, one of the primary points of reconciliation is understanding your true identity and that you are beloved by God. As you learn of who you really are, it is also necessary to grieve your father wound and journal your losses as you work through to forgiveness.

With both the mother and father wound, remember this is not an attack on how well your parents parented or how poorly they did. It is an acknowledgment that there may be things you needed but simply did not get. Every unmet need shows up somewhere in our lives, especially as business owners.

As you heal and mature in this area, you may find it meaningful to seek older men as business mentors. They can reflect the absent presence your soul has longed for; this, however, can only happen after you have done the work of understanding and owning your true identity as a daughter or son of God. Only then can the physical representations here on earth truly begin to mirror the reflections of Abba Father.

We mentioned the absence of a father could also invoke a lack of boundaries. While on a healing journey, ask a trustworthy friend to call you out for attention-seeking and flirtatious behaviors. Be aware of the transgenerational nature of the father wound: performance orientation (always striving for success to feel good about yourself), fighting authority and limits, and being emotionally unavailable, or angry. These behaviors are carried through in our parenting and mentoring of those following us.

Work on developing a rule of life that includes your personal mission, vision statement, and values. Develop SMART goals (SMART is an acronym for specific, measurable, achievable, relevant, and time-based). Utilize a daily to-do list and a weekly/monthly master list that you regularly review with a colleague, mentor, or coach. Remember to ask God to re-Father you! Your attachment to God as your Abba Father will guide your course.

Appendix B provides questions to explore your relationship with father (paternal) wounding, an invitation to go deeper, and an affirmation of alignment.

WOUNDS OF TRUST

There are very few things in life that can be done alone. In business, we need others, and if we are going to have a sustainable and profitable future, we need to be able to trust them.

If you have ever taken a class about human growth and development, you have probably heard of Erik Erickson's eight stages of psychosocial development. The gist of some of his profound theories includes an analysis of trust versus mistrust. His stages of psychosocial development build upon each other, and a problem in one stage impedes the progression to subsequent stages. He highlights trust as one of the first developmental tasks and the most important as we form our beliefs about ourselves and the world out of it. It addresses the question, Can I trust the people around me? And it builds hope into our worldview. Believe it or not, trust is accomplished in infancy. Its formation in infancy highlights that if our ability to trust was compromised during infancy, it is possible that we may still struggle to find others trustworthy today. If this is the case, you may find yourself plagued with nonspecific depression and unexplainable feelings of despair.

Infants whose caregivers do not meet their needs develop mistrust. They tend to have fearful personalities and prominent feelings of confusion and anxiety. They have difficulty entering and sustaining healthy relationships. They lack a strong social support system and lead lives of isolation and loneliness. This concept is valid even when the parents are trying to do everything they can to meet the infant's needs but may not know what is needed at the moment. In situations where infants are chronically sick with ear infections or colic and cannot be soothed, this can also cause a break in the trust dynamic. Wounds of trust and the inability to feel a sense of calm and security are not always due to negligence. While this is true, negligent or not, if it caused a wound, it is still a wound and must be addressed all the same.

Beyond wounds of trust developing during preverbal stages, the trust wound can also develop later during childhood from bullying and competition, during adolescence with painful rejection, failed romantic relationships, parental divorce, or other traumatic experiences. When trust is repeatedly violated, your mindset and whole worldview can turn negative and suspicious. You may come to the point of believing that everyone is out to get you and everyone has an ulterior motive. Trust wounds are exhausting and leave the wounded in a constant state of hypervigilance, wondering who will break their trust next.

It's also important to address that wounds of trust can come through betrayal, infidelity, or discovering a pattern of deceit in your loved one(s). Lisa Sinclair studied North American missionary women who had experienced marital sexual betrayal (Restoring the paths: Sexuality for Christian leaders, 2020). She found that ongoing deceit and a lack of voluntary and transparent disclosure were experienced as being far more painful than the actual deed(s) of betrayal. While this speaks to repeated relational infractions, the same is true when we have repeated business infractions that erode our trust. It is wound upon wound, upon wound—such profound pain.

When we experience trust wounds in infancy and again throughout our lives, these wounds of trust build upon the other, intensifying the deprivation and emotional response to the experience. It is not just the right now betrayal of our trust, but it is the wordless places that cannot describe the feelings of betrayal and desperation.

Unpacking Wounds of Trust

When trust is broken, it means that some expected and normal behavior or commitment was not met but violated. Those who have been neglected or abused may experience trust issues. Promises may have been habitually broken by an alcoholic parent or a loved one. Lies may have been told to cover addictions or financial impropriety. Wounds of trust happen when there is an expectation of another, and instead of seeing it fulfilled, we are let down in a big way, resulting in feelings of betrayal.

Wounds of trust aren't limited to our experiences with individuals; organizations also break trust. Law enforcement, legal systems, and medical providers fail to practice justly and with respect. Financial loss occurs through banking institutions, investment, and insurance failures. Your trust may have been eroded by systemic practices of racism or sexism in education and the workplace. Religious leaders break trust through moral failure, spiritual abuse, and breach of confidentiality. Churches betray with judgment, hypocrisy, and deceit. Our souls long for trust. Whether we experienced the trust wound in infancy or later, it is deeply disruptive to our growth, development, and overall well-being.

Wounds of Trust in Business

A trust wound provides you with a kind of truth meter. It is always on, vigilantly reading the situation, person, or business, always asking whether they are worthy of trust? You live with a high "index of suspicion," a medical phrase used for diagnosing a cluster of symptoms. Instead of diagnosing strep throat from a sudden fever and sore throat, you carefully watch for symptoms of dishonesty and lack of integrity. Is there exaggeration? Are promises kept? Any violation will make your distrust meter rise, and you will withdraw and possibly back out of the relationship or prospective deal.

If you have a trust wound, you prefer working alone and have trouble collaborating. You can count on yourself, but not others. Your team members may feel they cannot get close to you because it is hard to develop intimacy with someone on the alert and sensitive to imperfection. Everyone is on an angle, and you engage with them accordingly; the degree of their angle is the degree to which you've determined they can or cannot be trusted. If they mess up, the angle widens, and they are pushed further and further away from intimacy and engagement with you. This is not a conscious decision you are making; it is an automatic reflex.

Forbes, the American business magazine, asserted that no matter how great your product and your work, "Nothing is more important than trust. . . . Trust is the fabric that holds everything together" (2017, July 7). It is the foundation of cooperation. Our online business world, so complex and impersonal, requires trust, and it must be cultivated. Trust is key for collaboration, a safe and free exchange of ideas, an attitude of mutual respect, helping each other, and optimism.

Marvin K. Mayers, author of Christianity confronts culture (1987), noted that we need to answer the PQT, or prior question of trust, in every interaction. We have to consider "Is what I am doing, thinking, or saying building trust, or is it undermining trust?" The trust wound may so burrow in our soul that we become self-protective and defensive. Instead of looking to build trust in our life and business, we avoid risk and betrayal at all costs, to the great detriment of our life and business. Because of our woundedness, not only do we not trust others, but we too become difficult to trust.

If any of the following resonate with you, trust wounds may be a soul healing journey to explore. Breathe in each statement and observe how it feels when you read it.

- Commitment is challenging because it could all go bad.
- There is unexplained loneliness, sadness, or depression frequently in my life.
- Forgiving myself and others is not just hard; sometimes, it feels impossible.

A Soul in Business Biblical Balm for Wounds of Trust

When we are wounded, a balm brings healing. A balm offers soothing relief for wherever our ache is. We believe in the context of soul healing; there is no greater balm, no greater soothing element than the Word of God. Wounds of trust often happen because of other wounds mentioned in this book. If you have wounds from your parents, have experienced abuse, rejection, or lost something valuable, you will struggle with trust.

We were created for community and relationships with others. At its least, a lack of trust will be an insurmountable wall between you and the community and relationships you crave. Healing this wound is necessary.

A Kingdom Perspective of Trust
from LaTara Venise, Vision Activation Strategist

A person who has trust issues becomes jaded toward life in general. You see it in their actions, their attitude, and their behavior. You notice it in how they speak about life, you, and others. You find that the average entrepreneur dealing with trust wounds functions solo in just about all they do. Because they don't trust, they will work hard to do it all on their own. They are the ones who don't need help and can do it better themselves. If they happen to hire someone, they are most likely the micromanager, ensuring it's done exactly the way they want. To this business owner, everything is all good as long as they are in charge.

Really, what's happening is that this person has built walls as a result of the pain and trauma from one or more of the wounds mentioned in this book. Also, please remember the wounds discussed in this book are not exclusive, and there may be other wounds to deal with.

When one deals with trust issues and says they believe in God, they are essentially doing a disservice to the kingdom. The kingdom is about collaboration, connection, and community. It cannot be said enough; we were created for relationships, not to do things alone. Relationships must have levels of trust, and this trust should grow. Understandably, trust may sometimes be breached because we are human, but a wound of trust should never exist among God's children. There is work to be done, and one has to dig deep for the sake of their life and the continued existence of their business.

A Biblical Look at Healing Wounds of Trust

Most of us have a false perception of what it means to trust. As a result, we have walls and masks to hide the distrust we have. The funny thing is that it shows up. For one to begin to work on and heal the wounds of trust, they must tap into the reality of where trusting begins.

"Trust in the Lord with all your heart and lean not on your own understanding; in all your ways submit to him, and he will make your paths straight" (Proverbs 3:5–6 NIV).

Trusting any man without trusting God first can cause more damage than one knows. It's why our world is turned upside down. We look to man rather than God for someone to trust in. Now, this is not to say that you can't trust people. What I am saying is that we must first place our trust in the One who can guide us toward the right people, people we can, in turn, trust.

When we trust in him with all of our hearts, we find our hearts become more inclined toward the things of the Lord. If we are more inclined toward the heart of the Father, then our trust blooms into one that aligns with his.

Here are a few things you can begin to do to shift your perspective and perception of trust:

- Surrender all that you are. It is in surrender that you will learn the heart of the Father.
- Lean not to your own understanding. Instead, align your understanding with his wisdom. His wisdom will guide you to trust with his heart.
- Acknowledge him in all that you do. Whether at home, work, or elsewhere, acknowledge that God is the one who knows all, sees all, and has all power in his hands. You will

see how he shows up in your life and how much you can trust him.

Proper alignment of trust and how it operates in your life will direct every path you are called to embark upon. Rebuilding and learning to trust by putting one foot in front of the other and taking it step by step. One thing you can count on is that God is trustworthy. You can depend on him to keep his word concerning you. You can know without a doubt that he has your best interest in mind and desires to give you an expected end according to his Word (Jeremiah 29:11 KJV).

The Journey of Healing Wounds of Trust

Trust can indeed be destroyed in an instant, but it can take a lifetime to rebuild. The absence of trust in your business engagement and life endeavors is not one to be taken lightly. This is a soul wound that needs professional help and community to heal. We must learn to trust again. It is a skillful dance of vulnerability, rupture (something that happens that breaks our trust), and repair (we allow the trust wound to be healed in a timely fashion).

It is okay to engage in perceptive trust, meaning until you grow deeper in your trust journey, you trust others to the degree to which your soul believes they are trustworthy. Perhaps you try the journey of building trust with a counselor or therapist. They are trained to develop trust with others, honor boundaries, communicate clearly, and keep their word. Let them know that you see the world through eyes of mistrust and want that to change. Share with them the ways in which you are aware your trust has been broken while also considering that your wound of trust may even be preverbal.

All you know is that it is difficult to trust anyone, and you don't fully understand why.

You can also begin taking little risks toward trust with those close to you by sharing your vulnerability. Learn to speak in "I" statements: When you change our appointment, I feel that you don't want to be with me. When you exaggerated about that, I was afraid that you lie to me about other things. When you own the feelings that are happening inside you, you allow the other person to respond and provide you with information that may help you understand their behavior and thus help you identify if your feelings are related to their behavior or if there is hypervigilance at play causing you to struggle with trusting them.

In Beyond Boundaries: Learning to trust again, coauthored by John Townsend, he mentions "whatever your loss or whatever your hurt, you are designed to live in relationships, to reconnect and to be vulnerable—your difficulties can be redeemed and your self-protection resolved if you move in the right paths" (Townsend, 2011). The right path involves acknowledging and grieving your trust losses, setting boundaries with those who have broken your trust, and slowly taking intentional risks.

Healing the trust wound requires patience and grace for yourself and others. Living in a constant state of being on edge or, as the phrase goes, waiting on the other shoe to drop is exhausting. It is likely that you are physically, mentally, spiritually, and emotionally tired of constantly doing a risk assessment of the people around you and their propensity to lie, betray, or let you down. Make space for rest and low-pressure connections. These are connections with others where the stakes aren't high, you don't have to be on guard, and you can engage with them on a mutual level of trust and understanding. You are not an island, and you need people; equally important, people need you. Yes, others can be trusted.

Appendix C provides questions to explore your relationship with wounds of trust, an invitation to go deeper, and an affirmation of alignment.

WOUNDS OF ABUSE

The abuse wound creates an incomprehensible hole in our soul. We are created in the image of God, worthy of love and respect, yet someone has harmed us deeply. Good Therapy (goodtherapy. org) defines abuse as "a misuse of power intended to harm or control another person." The abused one feels powerless, unlovely, unworthy, shameful, bad, ugly, and deserving of abuse.

You may have taken a long road to come to terms with what happened to you and to call it abuse. To lessen the pain of the impact of abuse, we often find ourselves using old rationalizations:

- It wasn't that bad.
- He didn't mean it.
- She couldn't help herself.
- I invited it by talking back. By the way I dressed. By being too fat. By not understanding.

You may even notice you react strongly to being called a victim because it triggers feelings of powerlessness that you fight so fiercely against. Or you may have accepted a victim mentality and way of life, meaning not going against the current, being agreeable, being careful not to assert your real thoughts and feelings for fear of incurring displeasure. Unfortunately, many people only look at the "big" abuse wounds as abuse, but abuse can manifest itself in many forms and cause severe wounding to our personality and development.

Anxiety, anger, rage, and shame are natural emotional states for a survivor of abuse. As a professional and business owner, you have likely learned how to mask these feelings to function and manage your business the best you can. However, you may be aware you feel anxious in relationships and new situations and anxious in times of vulnerability and intimacy. You experience a lot of anger at past abusers, those who knew of your abuse and didn't intervene, and those who remind you of abusers (this is called transference and can contaminate current relationships). Most of all, you are angry at yourself for not getting away from your abuser. You have critical self-talk: You should have known! You should have fought back! You should have escaped! The abuse wound causes us to feel shame about our abuse as if it was our fault. On a deep level, you may be angry with God, who you feel didn't protect you.

For some of you, your abuse resulted in mental health problems like anxiety and depression. You may self-harm in ways that reenact the abuse. You may have post-traumatic stress disorder. PTSD is a psychiatric diagnosis with exacting criteria. In short, you experienced great danger, and the experience overwhelmed your ability to cope with it. Long after, you are still re-experiencing the abuse through memories, triggers, flashbacks, and nightmares. You see the world differently and darkly. You experience high arousal, have sleep problems, startle easily, and are irritable, anxious, and easily angered. You feel numb emotionally and detached from life and the world. You avoid things that remind you of the abuse. Not all abuse victims experience PTSD, and your cluster of symptoms will be unique to you. PTSD complicates abuse recovery and healing but can be part of your journey to wholeness.

It is worth seeking a mental health diagnosis if you sense you may have lingering effects from the abuse. This is not to put a label on yourself, but it is to know what you are dealing with so you can strategically address it. As a business owner, you mustn't allow the stigma of having a diagnosis to prevent you from being healed from the disorder.

Unpacking Wounds of Abuse

Abuse is injuring another intentionally or through neglect. There are four main types of abuse: physical, emotional, neglect, and sexual abuse. We can differentiate further types of abuse based on our own experience: spiritual abuse, mental abuse, verbal abuse, domestic abuse, financial abuse, institutional abuse, and cultural abuse, for example. Abuse occurs across a power differential—the more powerful harming the weaker—creating a perpetrator and a victim. When we think of abuse as a misuse of power, it is clear that abusers themselves often have been abused or are operating out of some habitual pattern. Consider the following:

- Not having heat, warm water, or enough food as a child— this is neglect, which is abuse.
- Being inappropriately touched or sexualized as a child by someone three years or older than you, even if they are also a child— this is sexual abuse.
- Having scars, red marks, or bruises from being hit as a child or adult— this is physical abuse.
- Being called derogatory names, yelled at, or cursed at— this is verbal abuse.
- Being manipulated by a pastor or spiritual leader to give large amounts of money or commit an unreasonable

amount of time and made to feel unworthy if you don't comply— this is spiritual abuse.

Abuse can be healed, but it is not as straightforward as healing a physical wound. It is not as easy as putting a cast on a limb and waiting for the bones to heal or as easy as stitching up an open wound. The lingering impact of abuse is often not seen. It is the unseen turmoil experienced in the heart, mind, and soul of the one who has experienced the abuse. Often those around them, if not aware of their history, have no idea the extent to which they struggle to engage in simple everyday tasks due to their experience.

Wounds of Abuse Business

When you were abused, you were put in the victim role and placed at a disadvantage along a power gradient. You were the weak or powerless one. Accordingly, you are very sensitive to power dynamics in relationships and in business. You have an instant radar that not only goes up but responds instinctively; you react negatively to any sense of control or power being exerted over you. You tend to perceive others as controlling when they simply assert their thoughts, opinions, or desires. As such, you may become controlling as you try to control the controllers around you. This cycle can make for exhausting business encounters.

You might be vulnerable to being taken advantage of, doing too much for others, and not establishing good work boundaries and responsibilities for your team. You may find yourself in codependent relationships and partnerships where you are always the caretaker. You are likely to struggle with self-care, giving away your needs in the service of others. Or you may rigidly defend your self-care boundaries for fear that someone will violate them. If you carry the abuse wound, you probably struggle with assertiveness. You can be nonassertive or even too aggressive. Instead of being direct in your communication, your natural default in conflict will be passive-aggressive.

If you have not addressed your experience of abuse, you likely have unexplained business blocks that you don't have words for. This is also attributed to the notion that some experiences of abuse happen before we have developed the part in our brain that allows us to put words to experiences. Sometimes the abuse may have been so severe that to survive, you have blocked it out altogether. Even if you have blocked it, if there is something in you feeling triggered as you read this, it is likely triggering and manifesting in your business as well.

A Soul in Business Biblical Balm for Wound of Abuse

When we are wounded, a balm brings healing. A balm offers soothing relief for wherever our ache is. We believe in the context of soul healing; there is no greater balm, no greater soothing element than the Word of God. As we have shared, abuse is not merely a physical manifestation of violence. Abuse of any kind will leave residual effects that will undoubtedly cause occupational hazards in your business if not addressed and healed.

While perhaps you could not control the experiences of abuse that happened to you, it's important to embrace the invitation you now have to heal how the abuse has hindered you.

Abuse and the Triggers of Low Self-Worth
from LaTara Venise, Vision Activation Strategist

The roots and issues surrounding wounds of abuse are more what the message of abuse is and not the act or behavior. The message that finds itself interwoven into abuse is "not worthy." A message of not being worthy can show up in business in several ways.

I was in a narcissistically controlling relationship for ten years, and it did not exactly begin without its struggles. I came into the relationship depressed and low, with an expectation that this man would give me all he promised, only to realize I would experience the exact opposite within the first twenty-four hours of landing in Chicago. However, I chose to stay, and it directly affected every aspect of who I was, even my business. My focus was off. I was pricing my offers too low, missing deadlines, creating more work than necessary, and losing clients consistently. As a result of feeling worthless and like there was not much I could do right, I inadvertently added this mindset and heart posture to how I conducted my business.

When you try to run a business with unattended wounds of abuse, it can also show up as a lack mindset. This lack mindset will, in turn, cause the entrepreneur to do much like I did—procrastinate to the point of self-sabotage. Anyone who has gained the victory of self-sabotage knows that this path leads to sabotaging people, places, and things. Your business will not benefit a soul; therefore, it will not benefit your soul.

The business owner who struggles with wounds of abuse must take the time to address the triggers that cause feelings of low self-worth that lead to procrastination and self-sabotage. It's difficult work, but once we understand and believe our value in God, it changes one's entire mindset.

A Biblical Look at Healing the Wounds of Abuse

"I praise you because I am fearfully and wonderfully made; your works are wonderful, I know that full well" (Psalm 139:14 NIV).

The day I tried to take my life in 2008, God was clear that it is not in his design or purpose that any of his children die by way of suicide. He was clear that he whispers his love for each of them, but that ultimately it's their choice. That day was the day when I began the healing process, and it started with a Scripture he gave me. It was a familiar message and one I had heard over and over again. However, it was not until that day that it became real to me.

Psalm 139:14 states something that I think many miss. This is why reading various versions of the Word is key. The latter part of this Scripture reveals exactly what God thinks of us. It states, "Your works are wonderful; I know that full well."

When one is dealing with healing from wounds of abuse, it is imperative that they understand, first, the value and measure of their being. God values us enough to make each of us at our very best. He places nothing worthless in us. Sin does that. Our Father's works are wonderful, and we are his workmanship. The problem with reading a Scripture like this is that we often glance over how to walk out the truth of our wonderful design. David stated that he knew "full well" that the works of God are wonderful.

Abuse can suffocate the ability to affirm who you are, but God gives us the right to affirm who we are in him. As you work at healing the wounds of abuse, you must take hold of the wonderful work you are. That's the key—you have to believe what you read and walk it out, knowing full well, like David, that when God created you, there were no mistakes. This takes work, but understand that you are empowered to heal and walk out the fact that you are a wonderful creation.

If you want more proof of your worth and value in God's eyes, you can read Psalm 139 as a complete love letter from God. In reading, you find no less than twenty reasons why God loves you and created you as a wonderful work. For the sake of time, I will list just two of the reasons here.

- God protects and covers what he loves and created. "You hem me in behind and before, and you lay your hand upon me" (Psalm 139:5 NIV).
- God loves you so much that he searches you, knows your every thought, and course corrects your heart and mind to be more like his. "Search me, God, and know my heart; test me and know my anxious thoughts. See if there is any offensive way in me, and lead me in the way everlasting" (Psalm 139:23–24 NIV).

When you get that you are a wonderful and marvelous work, you move differently. When you get that your Creator did not just make you, he also loves you; it shifts your heart.

The Journey of Healing Wounds of Abuse

The first step in healing is to acknowledge that what happened to you was wrong. Call it abuse! You did not deserve it; it was not your fault. Not just surviving abuse but thriving on the other side usually requires therapeutic help. In The healing path: How the hurts in your past can lead you to a more abundant life (2000), Dan Allender describes your suffering as a sacred journey of healing to greater wholeness. Allender is a prolific writer in sexual abuse recovery and offers weeklong treatment programs (see theallendarcenter.org). There are many good books and workbooks available to help you on your journey.

Because depression and anxiety are likely problematic for you, you may want to talk with your counselor and medical provider about antidepressant therapy. These medications are not addictive but treat your depleted brain chemicals and help your God-given neurocircuitry function more effectively. Medication may not be forever, but it may be necessary as you process and heal from some of the harsh realities of your experiences. Healing from abuse and processing this wound should not be taken lightly and without the supervision of a licensed and trained professional. Exercise is an important part of your healing because it gives you a sense of control over your body and functions as a God-given antianxiety and antidepressant agent.

Bessel van der Kolk, the pioneer of PTSD treatment, has written an important book, The body keeps the score (2014). Although your body may not speak with verbal words, it holds memories and pain and is key to your healing. You may be encouraged to engage in work that joins your mind and body together, like EMDR (eye movement desensitization and reprocessing) and EFT (emotional freedom technique) tapping. Research has shown relaxation exercises and rhythmic breathing to be helpful in PTSD and abuse recovery. Do not be discouraged by the length or depth of your healing journey. Allow it to draw you to God and his purpose for you. Remember to find time to play as you work through painful memories. Your business will thank you, and you will thank you too.

Appendix D provides questions to explore your relationship with wounds of abuse, an invitation to go deeper, and an affirmation of alignment.

WOUNDS OF REJECTION

Rejection hurts. It can start as early as the womb and continue its sting until our death. Rejection can be part of our early mother and father wounds. It can be the secret heart's cry of adopted children, the pain of not being picked for school teams, the pain of dating rejections, the longing for marriage, or the harshness of childhood cliques. Rejection wounds profoundly.

Dr. Ramona Woods (2010, June) often discusses the cycle of rejection as:

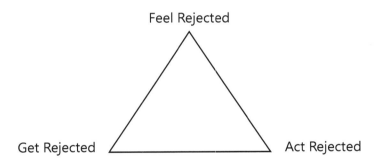

The unhealed rejection wound can turn to bitterness and hate. I will reject you before you reject me. It can also be internalized so that we reject and punish ourselves. In this model, we experience a feeling of perceived rejection that may or may not be true. However, because we feel the rejection, we, in turn, begin to act on the rejection. Acting rejected may look like isolating, not returning phone calls, and assuming you aren't wanted around even if others extend an invitation. Eventually, this behavior leads us to actually being rejected, which is what we wanted to avoid in the first place. Rejection is a brutal cycle where once the seed has been planted, it must be intentionally uprooted, healed, and replaced by feelings of love, acceptance, and presence.

There are many reasons people experience rejection. Often the people who feel rejection the deepest are the most creative, talented, brightest souls that exist. Their giftedness and talents can make them feel different. Feeling different can begin the dance into the cycle of feeling rejected, acting rejected, getting rejected. While this is one spectrum to look at, we must also mindfully explore that highly gifted and talented people do experience true rejection. This rejection, however, is not because of something deficient in them. Humans generally reject or question what they do not understand and often what they cannot control.

Observe if any of the following phrases bring up anything for you:

- You are the black sheep.
- You are too different.
- You are too much.
- You think you're better than us.
- You are hard to deal with.

If any of those phrases caused an emotional response or even a pause, you have likely experienced rejection from people close to you. Parents, siblings, cousins, and extended family members can ignite feelings of rejection in family members who don't go with the status quo, who may have a different interest than the majority of the family, and those with unique callings and giftings in their lives. Without going any further, if you have managed your own business, corporate success, or any great accomplishment, this is likely due to a unique calling on your life and the gift that is necessary to fulfill that calling. With that being said, it is a fair evaluation that because of this, you have experienced and responded to feelings of rejection in your life.

Unpacking Wounds of Rejection

Rejection means that we are not chosen or wanted; we are not considered worthy. It is the proclamation that something is wrong with us. We are refused actively or passively. We are not good enough, repulsed because of who we are or who we are not. We are rejected because of how we look, our color, our weight, our hair. We are rejected because of our culture or ethnicity, religion, sexual orientation, or gender identity. We are rejected because of our style, friends, accomplishments, accent, or intelligence.

Rejection leaves scars that affect how we view ourselves and life itself. We become on guard, fearful of, and vigilant for rejection; we become what the therapeutic community calls "rejection sensitive." Our experience of rejection and fear of further rejection creates an unfortunate spiral. We react, withdraw, expect more rejection, and thus become magnets for it.

The rejection wound causes ongoing suffering as we undervalue ourselves and expect little from those around us. Solitude is preferable to the risk of rejection, and our life can be marked by loneliness and avoidance of others. We doubt positive affirmation; compliments, invitations, and inclusion are met with suspicion and disbelief. Eventually, we become more comfortable with rejection than with acceptance.

Wounds of Rejection in Business

If you have managed to function despite your painful soul wound of rejection, you may still encounter and battle difficult barriers in your business. Because of the rejection wound, you tend to work alone and don't easily or willingly collaborate with others. In communication, you are either introverted or people-pleasing, but never just yourself. You stay busy and are perfectionistic. You consciously and unconsciously avoid the risk of rejection. You do not want to stand out with creative ideas or innovations that reveal who you are and open you up to criticism and rejection. You are not a team player. Shame, that sense of being bad will bind your true self-desires. All the dreams and possibilities of your work are paralyzed under the deadening effects of the cloud of rejection.

Wounds of rejection in business will cause you to hold back a multimillion-dollar idea, book, brand, or product out of fear that it is not good enough or will not be well received or accepted. The other side of rejection will cause fear on What if it is accepted and received? How will I maintain this acceptance? Fear of succeeding becomes rejection's bed partner, and the death gripping fear to maintain the success or the acceptance becomes too much to bear.

A Soul in Business Biblical Balm for Wounds of Rejection

When we are wounded, a balm brings healing. A balm offers soothing relief for wherever our ache is. We believe in the context of soul healing; there is no greater balm, no greater soothing element than the Word of God. The wound of rejection is perhaps one of the most painful soul wounds to exist. It targets the core of who you are, and it screams, You are not enough!

Rejection can strip the fibers of our soul. It becomes difficult to imagine that you are not only enough, but you were uniquely designed as you are for a purpose, and the world would not be the same without you. That's how necessary you are, just the way you are.

The Depth of Rejection
from LaTara Venise, Vision Activation Strategist

Dismissed. Inadequate. Inconvenient. I am the youngest of eight children, and let's just say that I don't have real relationships with any of my siblings. My story with these folks has been one of rejection and abandonment that led me to become more functional in relationships in an effort to help me feel needed. As long as people needed me to do something, I felt wanted and loved. It was how I built relationships, but this type of effort to be loved and wanted only causes other issues.

As a result of the rejection I struggled with and the way I showed up in relationships, I was closed off, exhibited a tough demeanor, and created walls as my typical mode of operation. As an entrepreneur, the reaction to the wound of rejection showed up the same way. I took on additional work, even if my plate was full. I hustled to balance the plate, and something always seemed to spill over. That's when I would create a new wall, calling it a boundary. I sabotaged many projects, procrastinated on things to be done, and often ran from what God told me I needed to get done.

It was easier to cause a void and create walls of division based on false perceptions instead of dealing with the root causes of my rejection. Honestly, until 2019, I was not really aware of just how deep this wound was. I attended a prophetic retreat, and

God healed me in such a way that the walls came down, my heart opened up to developing real relationships. I learned how to love my siblings without any expectation of deeper relationships. Even how I showed up in business changed. I created safe boundaries, emptied my plate of what did not work, and moved forward without needing to function as a jack-of-all-trades for my clients.

A Biblical Look at Healing Wounds of Rejection

Are you tired? Worn out? Burned out on religion? Come to me. Get away with me and you'll recover your life. I'll show you how to take a real rest. Walk with me and work with me—watch how I do it. Learn the unforced rhythms of grace. I won't lay anything heavy or ill-fitting on you. Keep company with me and you'll learn to live freely and lightly." (Matthew 11:28–30 MSG)

The only healing source for rejection is to be loved in the right way—unconditionally. I love the words of the Scripture above. Here Jesus reminds us just how much he loves us. He also gives us a remedy for dealing with the wound of rejection. "Simply join your life with mine."

Dealing with wounds of rejection causes clutter, confusion, and an overwhelming feeling of being abandoned. Jesus desires to do life with us. He wants to ease our pain, and the heaviness life can often bring. Rejection is not the way of the kingdom. We are welcome as children of God and heirs of the kingdom. When we take the opportunity to do life with Jesus, he eases the burdens that wounds of rejection cause. Instead, he offers us refreshment and rest for our lives. "For the Lord will not forsake his people; he will not abandon his heritage" (Psalm 94:14 ESV).

If rejection is your wound, God is your healer. His ability and willingness to love you beyond measure can heal your heart if you allow it. His goal is to receive you, not make you feel inadequate. Our Father created you with great purpose. He desires to see you win, and he knows that it is in his presence that you do so.

God's soul presence and acceptance as Abba Father is the only sufficient balm for the soul wound of rejection.

The Journey of Healing Wounds of Rejection

Just as with the other soul wounds, the scars of rejection are not easily or quickly healed. Confession and forgiveness will be key in renouncing the spirit of rejection and shame that so effectively bind you and have marred your God-given giftedness, purpose, and identity. But first, you must feel the pain. Take time to journal all the experiences of rejection that you can remember. Take them to God and allow yourself to feel the full pain of each instance. Cry because tears are healing. Yell or scream (in a way that won't frighten your neighbors) and let your pain be released unto the Lord, who understands rejection. Let yourself feel the pain of shame and self-hatred, and bitterness. This process will be more effective with the help of a counselor who can help you combat intense feelings of self-hatred and the triggers to self-medicate and numb.

Rejection is a common experience of life. Because of rejection's hole in your heart, you are easily triggered to traumatic places of pain. Use life's lighter stings to practice self-acceptance and love. For example, imagine putting a stiff arm out before you and saying, This is you. You reject me because of XYZ. Then you bring your hand against your chest and say, This is me. I am a child of

God, chosen and beloved. Continue the dialogue and stiff-arming the other while embracing your heart until you feel the peace of self-acceptance and detachment from the rejecting messages of the other. In this exercise, you detach from the fear of man and the profound need for others' approval. You strengthen your own voice and your ability to affirm and protect yourself appropriately. You can practice this at home and in privacy and then enact the scenario silently when the real rejection happens. As long as we live among humanity, it will happen, and you can survive it.

As you heal, you gain insight into the shaming behavior of others and discover the reality of their own shame-based rejection histories. As you learn to tell yourself the truth and question critical self-talk, you uncover many lies that you have believed about yourself. You learn to tell yourself the truth, anchoring yourself to God's appraisal of you. William Backus and Marie Chapian have a classic book to help you with this, Telling yourself the truth: Find your way out of depression, anxiety, fear, anger and other common problems by applying the principles of misbelief therapy (2001). Slowly, as you accept yourself, grieve your pain, and forgive your offenders, roots of healthy self-esteem develop.

Curt Thompson, a psychiatrist, has written The soul of shame (2015). He encourages us to seek out shame where it hides by noting occurrences on a three-by-five-inch card that you carry with you to notice its occurrence without giving it power by analyzing. He emphasizes the importance of a healing community where shame is put to death together. As your recovery continues, you will emerge from the shadows into the light where your business can truly bless the world.

Appendix E provides questions to explore your relationship with wounds of rejection, an invitation to go deeper, and an affirmation of alignment.

WOUNDS OF LOSS

When loss is experienced, whether it is a person, home, job, relationship, or favorite item, it is necessary to acknowledge it. Terry Wardle says, "Every loss deserves to be grieved, whether you've lost your favorite person or your favorite pen." The reality is we don't live in a society that welcomes the opportunities necessary to pause and experience all of the feelings associated with loss. We live in a pick-up-and-keep-moving society. The rush of our daily lives, the striving for more, the reality that often there just isn't time for us to stop and be in the moment. The truth is there isn't time not to stop and be in the moment.

When we don't take the necessary moments to process our lives, eventually, the moments begin to catch us in the most inopportune times. While it really may be necessary for us to be fully engaged in an event or with a client, we notice we cannot because our minds and hearts have drifted off to what we have not attended to.

Loss is the experience of having something at one moment and no longer having it at the next moment. When loss is abrupt and unexpected, it can be devastating. When loss is expected and prolonged, it can be gut-wrenching. In surveying people who have lost loved ones suddenly or in an expected loss, neither express a preference; their only heart's desire is not to have the loss at all. They long for what once was to be again. Even if there is time to prepare, it does not prevent or change the outcome.

Loss is loss and must be grieved.

The acknowledgment of loss must also be extended when a relationship is dissolved beyond reconciliation; that, too, feels like a death, and it too must be grieved. Beyond losing people we love, can be the loss of things and even experiences. Sudden losses can come from life events, such as house fires, company closures, and even theft.

Every single loss must be grieved. This cannot be overstated.

The psychology of grief lists five stages of grief as denial, anger, bargaining, depression, and acceptance. These stages don't go in order, and they aren't restricted to a particular timeframe, nor do they guarantee not to resurface and modulate between stages. Grieving can find you angry one moment, deep into the throes of depression in the next moment, and landing at acceptance before it is over. This process is unique to each individual and unique to every experience of loss.

Throughout this work, we have explored various wounds that no doubt leave a profound loss in our souls and must be grieved as well. Consider, if you have found areas of healing needed in the mother wound, father wound, wounds of trust, wounds of abuse, or wounds of rejection, that each of these wounds also brought along with it a measure of loss from innocence to absence. Not many escape this wound, and you are not alone in the deep grief it fosters.

When loss happens, and we are put in a position to figure out what happens next, this can create scarcity and a fear-based perspective in life. Many who lost caretakers early didn't receive the proper support for grieving the loss or were forced into maturing early. So they may be more resistant to taking risks and more likely to hoard or hold on to everything they have out of fear of losing again. The fear of losing again can prevent developing or sustaining friendships, limit growth, and stifle vulnerability.

Unpacking Wounds of Loss

The loss wound slows you mentally. It affects your immunity, your cardiovascular and gastrointestinal systems and even shortens your lifespan. It is the deprivation of something or someone of value that we once had access to and is now out of reach. It creates distance in your relationships and is extremely tiring. It may cause you to doubt God's character—His goodness, love, power, and knowledge of your situation. Although loss is common to all of us, some of us struggle because the nature of the loss caused us complicated grief, as in a child or sudden violent death.

When our loss is not acknowledged, it adds to the grief. Being forced to bear a secret loss such as a miscarriage or a loved one with dementia can complicate our grieving process as we bear them silently. For some, the wounds of loss represent the slow erosion in our soul due to the continual and accumulated losses we have experienced (for example, chronic disease, poverty, the stresses of racism, the lack of support as a single parent, etc.). With the wound of loss, we struggle with despair and have difficulty re-engaging with life and relationships.

Wounds of Loss in Business

The soul wound of loss depresses your natural giftedness. It deadens your enthusiasm for work and decreases your creativity and innovation. You are disinterested in team building and relationships. You lack the energy to address conflicts or to enthuse your colleagues. If a long accumulation of loss marks your life, you might have a mindset of lack; you might not believe in the concept of going after more, much less the impossible. You do not have the emotional bandwidth to commit to new relationships or intimacy, and you withdraw to protect yourself from vulnerability and further loss. You do not inspire confidence within your team nor trust in your clients. Your ability to work is muffled. Depression prevents your business from thriving. The loss wound is a big obstacle to fulfillment and success.

Your business will either stagnate or fail without healing this soul wound. Remember, every loss deserves to be acknowledged and grieved. Consider whether the following losses resonate with you.

- a phone or electronic device with photos or irreplaceable documents
- a loved one's death
- a loved one lost due to necessary boundaries
- perspective, vision, passion
- joy
- yourself
- financial investments
- business collaboration
- home or car

A Soul in Business Biblical Balm for Wounds of Loss

When we are wounded, a balm brings healing. A balm offers soothing relief for wherever our ache is. We believe in the context of soul healing; there is no greater balm, no greater soothing element than the Word of God. Wounds of loss grip the heart and emotions; it requires permission to feel every ounce of grief in the soul. Loss is healed best in the presence of a community that will hold the space for you to process the pain and to simply be present.

It's important to note that even when we experience unimaginable losses, restoration is available. God in His sovereignty may replace, and in His love, He always restores.

A Personal Relationship with Loss
from LaTara Venise, Vision Activation Strategist

I have suffered a great deal of loss in my life, but I don't think anything prepared me for what happened within an eight-day period in 2015. On September 18, we lost our home to fire. Six days later, my oldest living nephew was shot and killed. Imagine the struggle. Imagine the trauma. Imagine the loss.

We lost so many precious memories and things. It was as if we had been disconnected from life, and when my nephew was murdered that next week, I could barely fathom what life looked like. It was a day-by-day, often minute-by-minute process to simply open my eyes and get through the day. I stopped coaching for two months because I was no good to anyone. Many days, getting out of bed was hard and unbearable. Breathing above my tears proved to be difficult because my emotions often won the battle, and there were days I could not stop crying.

Wounds of Loss Roots and Issues

The main root of a wound of loss is fear. I'm often reminded of my mother when I think of the fear of loss. My mother was born seven years after the Great Depression. She was a Black woman whose people had not even been free for 100 years. She was a part of the generation where they had to grab hold of what was necessary before it was no longer available. As a result, my mother became a hoarder of many things, especially food. I remember when I moved to Oklahoma in 2009, there was ketchup that had been on the shelf for so long it had turned brown. When I asked her why she had so many and some were brown, she told me that she hates running out of things. Over the last twelve years, she has gotten better, but she still tries to save as much as she can, even when I fuss about it.

It's important to note that as a business owner, my mother's story is one that might be yours too.

If you struggle with deleting old unnecessary files, signing up for a multitude of freebies, attending every webinar, even having more than maybe two coaches at a time, you are likely suffering from a wound of loss. That's one of the main issues of this wound; it causes you to hoard, and hoarding leads to many other mental, physical, and emotional issues.

Another issue that pops up for the business owner dealing with a wound of loss is the tendency to build walls and call them boundaries. It becomes a norm for many who struggle with loss to create unhealthy blocks that lead to irrational behavior. Boundaries that are truly healthy focus on solutions that help maintain sanity in the lives of everyone involved.

A Biblical Look at Healing the Wound of Loss

In any issue with loss, it is important to note that restoration is God's answer.

God does not take, he adds. Even if something is removed that does not belong, he replaces it with what does belong. Restoration is his specialty.

From the day in 2015 when the fire took my home until this very moment, I have watched how God restores, even when you can't fathom how you will survive. Over time I watched how God restored what was lost, and my family is now living in a truly abundant overflow.

> God, your God, will restore everything you lost; he'll have compassion on you; he'll come back and pick up the pieces from all the places where you were scattered. (Deuteronomy 30:3 MSG)

> Keep a cool head. Stay alert. The Devil is poised to pounce, and would like nothing better than to catch you napping. Keep your guard up. You're not the only ones plunged into these hard times. It's the same with Christians all over the world. So keep a firm grip on the faith. The suffering won't last forever. It won't be long before this generous God who has great plans for us in Christ—eternal and glorious plans they are!—will have you put together and on your feet for good. He gets the last word; yes, he does. (1 Peter 5:8-11 MSG)

God does a few things during the restoration process that should help the business owner heal from this wound to be encouraged in knowing all that seems lost is actually not.

- **God will restore.** His restoration is always better. Consider Job. After losing property, servants, and children, he probably never imagined getting any of it back. But God, in his sovereignty, saw fit to restore all that was lost, and Job

75

was blessed with more than he originally had: his property, servants, and children. (Read Job chapters 1 and 42.)

- **God will pick up.** Whatever broken pieces are left after loss—God picks them up for you. You don't have to do a thing but trust the process he takes you through, and much like Job, you will see even the broken pieces will be used. There is nothing wasted with God.

- **God will set up.** Matthew 6:33 in The Message translation tells us that we need to "steep" ourselves in "God-initiative." That means that we need to posture and position ourselves for what our loving Father has already established. After loss, position yourself in his will. He has already established what is needed for you.

- **God will support.** The bottom line is that God loves you and wants the best for you. He did not create you to bring harm to you. (That's how Satan works.) Jesus tells us in John 10:10 that the purpose of the kingdom and his coming is to bring life—an abundant life. The enemy comes to kill, steal, and destroy, but the kingdom provides for you and caters to you in ways you will never know if you keep the wound of loss open.

As you consider the healing of your business, don't think it to be a daunting task. Yes, there is work to be done. When you consider the restoration process and how our Father lovingly takes us through the process, you can see that you have already been empowered with everything you need to experience an abundant overflow in your life and business. Webster's dictionary says restoration is about reinstating or bringing back. It goes a step further with God because his restoration is kissed with his glory and love, causing that lost thing to be brand-new or the restoration of the loss in a new and unique way.

The Journey of Healing Wounds of Loss

To heal the loss wound, no matter its origins, you must engage in active grieving. This journey requires courage and perseverance. Set aside a weekend retreat to create your loss inventory. Use a poster board, post-it notes, and colored markers. Draw your lifeline from birth until today. Allow the line to follow your major ups and downs. Mark each hill and valley with an image or an explanatory post-it note. Use markers to section off chapters of your life and write a title for each chapter. When you have completed this timeline, take time to be with it. Ask God to walk through it with you and tell him about each loss that you have marked. You can also join us at healyourbusiness.academy and complete an experience like this together with us.

You must allow yourself time to feel the pain and cry until you have expressed the grief of each situation and loss. When you reach the end of your timeline, ask God to tell you how he sees your life with all these losses. Ask him to tell you what the meaning of your story is and what his purpose for you is. Commit your loss inventory and everything you think he is telling you to him. Take time to journal your experience. You may find that you are exhausted and achy after this activity, so take good care of yourself. Rest, drink lots of water, and eat a nutritious and healthy meal. In the days ahead, you will find that your life is no longer defined solely by loss. Life and purpose will gradually renew as you remember the rich chapters of your story, all gathering into his story for you. You will benefit from sharing your timeline with a therapist and a close group of friends who can support you in your loss wound recovery.

Unexplained suffering calls for faith in God's goodness. Timothy Keller helps us understand our loss wound theologically in his book, Walking with God through pain and suffering. What is grief and why does God allow suffering (2015). Allow Scripture to fill the void of your loss wound. Mark God's promises as you read them and claim them as your own. Journal about what God has given you now and what your inheritance is in him! You are a child of God, and he wants to lavish his love on you.

Appendix F provides questions to explore your relationship with wounds of loss, an invitation to go deeper, and an affirmation of alignment.

WOUNDS OF UNRESOLVED ISSUES

On some level, we all have wounds of unresolved issues. If you have experienced any of the other wounds mentioned in this work and have yet to address them fully, then guess what? They sit in your soul, your life, and your business as unresolved issues. Raising your level of awareness to this isn't to induce shame or guilt. Instead, it is to extend an invitation to address the things you know are there and no longer meander around like they don't exist. You have power, and you have support as you do the hard work.

It's important to acknowledge that it is not always negligence when we do not address unresolved issues. Often, we don't know how to do the work, we don't know who will support us while doing the work, and we have no idea what the work looks like. We are aware there is this thing that is disruptive in our lives, yet we may not know what to do with it.

In cases where we cannot name our unresolved issues, and perhaps our awareness of the issues is not as keen, there are ways to know if unresolved issues lurk under the surface. Unresolved issues tend to leave us with tender places in our emotional lives. You may experience an offense that on the surface, does not warrant the level of intensity you project as it is happening. It is likely because that offense touched an unresolved issue, and you are not only feeling the current wound but also feeling the wound under the wound. Therefore, it is so important to address issues as they arise and surrender deep wounds for healing. One of the dangers of avoiding unpacking our unresolved issues is the risk of responding to a simple wound based on a multi-layered wounded experience.

An example of this can be a team member who does not complete a task on time and slows down business operations. This is a justifiable infraction on the business. However, suppose there is a history of individuals not completing tasks or not showing up fully in the business. In that case, the business owner may be tempted to respond not only to this simple infraction but to give a harsh unloading to this one person for the last ten people who have missed a deadline or dropped the ball.

How did it feel to read that example? Notice it and acknowledge if you have responded this way in business or a life situation. The pileup often happens in intimate relationships as well. We are prone to just let things go, and then one day, the smaller thing reaps the mounting months or even years of offenses that were left unresolved and unaddressed.

Unresolved issues are akin to holding stuff in that needs to be released. Anything held inside the body that does not belong or needs to come out becomes toxic and eventually sets up an infection that could lead to death. In the same way, anything held inside your heart, mind, or soul that does not belong there, that needs to be purged out or released, will set up an infection and lead to emotional, spiritual, relational, entrepreneurial, and even physical death. We are not created to hold in toxicity; we are created to release it and live free. This is why the healing journey matters. It is the reason we found it necessary to pour out the words on these pages, to invite you into a self-exploration, an examination of where your soul may need to heal deeper.

We understand that many times we have already been committed to doing healing work. We have addressed our negative thought patterns. We have healed from what are considered the major wounds. However, wherever there is residue, there are unresolved issues, and these unresolved issues must be addressed for your soul and your business to thrive.

It's important to celebrate the healing you've already done, celebrate where you are, and be brave enough to go further. It's also important to note that healing happens in layers and is an ever-evolving journey. The deeper you heal, the more you become aware of the uniqueness and gifts that lie in the corridors of your mind. Along the journey, you may begin to identify that you are called to walk alongside another on a healing journey. It is impossible to walk and live in this freedom with unresolved issues lingering.

Unpacking Wounds of Unresolved Issues

Unresolved issues weigh us down. These are all the things we know about. The things we know have been wrong or hurtful. Things that have been woven into our identity in a way that we know distorts us. We haven't addressed them because we are afraid of what might happen. Maybe we will fall apart. Maybe we will go crazy. Perhaps if we change, we will lose the only security we have known—even though it is destructive. Maybe we think that we can do it tomorrow because we are too busy with important things today. Perhaps we've tried to address these things but have failed again and again to make any progress. Maybe we know that we can't do it on our own, but we are afraid to ask for help. Asking for help might mean to us that we don't believe in God, who ought to heal us without anyone else's help! Asking for help might bring about another's displeasure and judgment because they think we ought to be able to do it on our own or with God alone. Whatever the reasons, to allow unresolved issues to fester beneath the surface of your life is to deny yourself all God has for you, limiting your access to health and wholeness.

Unresolved issues form an enslaving chain, each link fused on by rationalization, denial, and avoidance. This chain weighs us down and restricts our movement, slowing our pace and keeping us from the joy of running ahead fully in purpose and prosperity!

Wounds of Unresolved Issues in Business

When we attempt to navigate business through the lens of unresolved issues, we are like a toddler on their first experience of out-of-home care. The goal is immediately to determine friend or foe and neutralize the threats. We are in a constant state of hypervigilance, and we are all over the place as we try to control our lives while avoiding the ever-present wound that interferes in unexpected places and ways. We are lost, desperately seeking connection and safety.

Unresolved issues cause old things to keep us from new things; old relationships and beliefs keep us from growth and intimacy. We live out the impostor syndrome, believing we don't deserve whatever good we are doing or getting. We sabotage our efforts and our business initiatives. Our emotions are all over the place, causing our team or colleagues to feel like they are walking on eggshells around us. Our leadership is inconsistent, creating anxiety in our workplace. We either hide in passivity, or we engage in risky, impulsive ventures. Unresolved issues form a wound that is lived out in being unreliable in our business pursuits.

Explore if any of the following emotions resonate with you. If they do, they are likely tied to an unresolved issue that needs to be addressed.

- fear
- anger
- sadness
- loneliness
- apathy
- frustration
- emptiness
- inadequacy
- guilt

A Soul in Business Biblical Balm for Wounds of Unresolved Issues

When we are wounded, a balm brings healing. A balm offers soothing relief for wherever our ache is. We believe in the context of soul healing; there is no greater balm, no greater soothing element than the Word of God. Unresolved issues alert us that something is not quite settled, and they are impossible to deny. At moments where our mind and heart are quiet, they speak loudly.

Healing unresolved issues begins with addressing them without shame or guilt but with acceptance and grace.

Getting to the Root of Unresolved Issues
from LaTara Venise, Vision Activation Strategist

When you consider that something is unresolved, you have to look at a few things:

- **Communication.** Often we struggle with unresolved issues because we simply don't talk things out. Fear causes us to avoid and ignore the signs that something is not quite settled. For some business owners, this may show up as passive-aggressive behavior or even people-pleasing in an attempt to keep the waters calm. Neither method works. Healthy communication is necessary.

- **Emotional Maturity.** A lack of communication is a clear indication of our level of emotional intelligence and maturity. When we struggle with being emotionally balanced, we will fail to see the unresolved issues as hindrances. Instead, what many of us do is emotional stacking: pack the emotions away to deal with another day. This type of behavior causes physical, mental, and emotional pain, showing up in how we do business.

- **Perceptions.** When we are not emotionally mature, we see things from a toxic perspective. We begin to perceive things based on negative emotions and the lies the enemy whispers in our ears. We then allow them to become integrated parts of how we think, breathe, and move, causing us to avoid necessary conversations because we fear what will happen and how we will be perceived.

A Biblical Look at Healing Wounds of Unresolved Issues

Let's explore what the Word says about healing from unresolved issues.

Healing unresolved issues will require some kind of communication. That communication may be a phone call, an in-person sit-down, or maybe a letter. I had unresolved issues with my father, but he had died by the time I recognized them. I had to sit down and communicate my issues via a letter that I still have. In the letter, I was honest about my pain while lovingly conveying what he meant to me. The latter part is important.

> "Let your conversation be always full of grace, seasoned with salt, so that you may know how to answer everyone" (Colossians 4:6 NIV).

The goal for anyone struggling with unresolved issues should be to settle them with the right speech, behavior, and actions. That takes work, but it can be done.

Right speech requires that we use words that express truth in love. That can be hard when dealing with unresolved issues that may manifest through anger, fear, or other negative emotions. The key is to make sure you are flavoring your words with the heart of God first; then, you will be able to share the words of the Father. This does not mean there will not be some necessary deep conversation, but it does mean that the way you have the conversation will be more productive. Nothing productive comes from operating and speaking out of fear or anger.

> "Finally, brothers and sisters, whatever is true, whatever is noble, whatever is right, whatever is pure, whatever is lovely, whatever is admirable—if anything is excellent or praiseworthy—think about such things" (Philippians 4:8 NIV).

Don't become so well-adjusted to your culture that you fit into it without even thinking. Instead, fix your attention on God. You'll be changed from the inside out. Readily recognize what he wants from you and quickly respond to it. Unlike the culture around you, always dragging you down to its level of immaturity, God brings the best out of you and develops well-formed maturity in you (see Romans 12:2 NIV).

In working on healing wounds of unresolved issues, both attitude and behavior must be considered. When we approach healing with bitter roots, then we really aren't healing. We are masking up and avoiding the inevitable. It is important to do the work to remove the bitter roots, carrying an attitude that will lead to the right behavior when we work at healing unresolved issues. Doing so will help you communicate with an emotional maturity that will help you gain clarity and resolution, even if all you can do is write a letter.

I want to note that anger may arise in healing the wound of unresolved issues. That's fine. Anger can be healthy and necessary when you need to get to the root of something unresolved. However, misplaced anger and especially when it is unprocessed, can be dangerous. The key is to make sure you carry the love of the Father with you even when you struggle with anger.

The Journey of Healing Wounds of Unresolved Issues

Most times, the unresolved issues wound is not hidden from us; we know about these things. Because of our awareness, this wound contributes to our load of shame, low self-esteem, and self-criticism. It is helpful to identify the things we are afraid of, and that trigger us. Why are we still carrying these chains? Take time to journal about your unresolved issues, naming them one by one. Note and acknowledge your fears about addressing these issues. Meet with a counselor, coach, or spiritual director to help identify a realistic plan to approach your life recovery. You will not be able to tackle everything at once; remember that healing and recovery are a lifetime journey.

As you address these old issues, practice an intentional balance of work, rest, and recreation. Remember that Einstein was a genius, and he defined insanity as doing the same thing over and over and expecting different results. Our little changes will reap big benefits and different results. Remember that you are housed in a body, and your body must take you everywhere you want to go, so taking good care of it is not optional. Incorporate rhythmic breathing, centering prayer, and progressive relaxation when anxiety grips you.

As you walk with the Lord through unresolved issues in your life, choose to become a master at confession and forgiveness, make it a daily practice. Adele Calhoun has written a very helpful guide. Spiritual disciplines handbook: Practices that transform us (2015) will help you match your unresolved issues and dysfunctional relating with healthy practices as antidotes. Allow yourself to admit how your unresolved issues wound has eroded your faith in God and his good and loving plan for your life.

Larry Crabb, psychologist, has written many helpful books that support the healing journey. In Shattered dreams: God's unexpected path to joy (2001), Crabb helps us see our healing journey from God's perspective. Our unresolved issues limit us to small worlds, small dreams, and unfulfilling relationships. Don't try to take this journey alone! We are created for community, and God heals through community. Ask God to help you find like-minded hearts in healing and recovery. Entrust Him with your healing. Remember that as your soul wounds heal, your business will heal, and God will be glorified through your life and your work.

Appendix G provides questions to explore your relationship with wounds of unresolved issues, an invitation to go deeper, and an affirmation of alignment.

HEALED IN SOUL & BUSINESS

Healing matters. You matter. Community matters. When we have the example of someone who has been on a journey, we have yet to travel, and when we watch them sojourn, it encourages us to move forward.

We not only want to invite you into our community, but we also want to introduce you to business owners who are healed and healing in soul and business. In the next section of this work, you will meet business owners who have experienced healing in their lives that manifested in their business or professional role. Through this healing, their business, relationships, and life continue to thrive!

In no way do we seek to imply that they or we have made an arrival, but we understand the commitment to a healing journey produces the lifetime transformation.

Why heal your soul?

- Unlock corridors in your mind where untapped creativity resides.
- Experience a depth of joy and peace that is unshakable.
- Live in a state of self-acceptance, self-awareness, and self-love that is a magnet to your target audience.
- Walk-in freedom that is not tied to or contingent upon anyone else or anything else around you.

- Become the gift of healing you've experienced for someone else.

Why heal your soul?

We'll let the following business owners share their stories, and you'll see the reasons are endless, and you are not alone on the journey.

A.J. Bussey, Founder & CEO

Business: 9ine Two 5ive LLC

Website: thefitpastor.org

Mission: 9ineTwo5ive exists to show young men that the value of life is in the paths we create and not the ones we follow. We look to encourage young men to become who they were created to be in whatever their passions are in an effort to make long-lasting, sustainable change in the communities around them. The purpose of 9ineTwo5ive is best explained in 1 Corinthians 9:25: "A true athlete will be disciplined in every respect, practicing constant self-control in order to win a laurel wreath that quickly withers. But we run our race to win a victor's crown that will last forever."

Bio: A Los Angeles native, A.J. grew up watching sports from the age of two, and his love for basketball and football never died. He started playing sports at age seven and went on through collegiate and minor league levels as well. Since leaving minor league football, he has continued his love of sports by writing for the Suave Report as a sports and culture contributor. He currently lives in Oklahoma City with his wife, Beth, and their 14-year-old.

How do you comprehend trauma and the impact it'll have on your life at age eleven? You don't. In fact, you don't comprehend it until you're ready to admit that you have wounds and scars that need healing. At age ten, I found out that I would receive the one thing I had waited my entire life for, a dad. I was so excited to have a father like many of my friends that I envied. But what I did not know was the seventeen-year struggle I was about to embark on. I was ten years old when my mother and I moved from Los Angeles to Chicago, and life was trending up—I thought. The picture that was painted for us was something you could compare to Van Gogh's The Siesta, a restful, peaceful portrait of love and contentment. Instead, my mother, brother, and I suffered an immense amount of abuse that would haunt us all for multiple years.

In the late summer of 2002, I came home from spending summer vacation at Granny's house and had some amazing news from my mom: She met someone, and we were going to move if I was okay with it. And of course, I was! I was a ten-year-old who was desperate to have a relationship with a father. In November of that year, we moved to Chicago, and our new life began. I was beyond excited for what lay ahead. For me, I would be able to finally see my dreams and my mom's dreams come to fruition. It was an opportunity for our family to be complete.

I'll never forget the first time my stepfather hit me. He hit me so hard my legs went numb, and I fell over. My stepfather took pleasure in knowing I feared him. It boosted his ego and allowed him to feel powerful and in control of the situation. I spent the next four years begging for his approval however I could gain it. I wanted to have his acceptance so bad I was willing to allow myself to become whoever he wanted me to be—even if that meant his verbal and physical punching bag. I was the only one he would hit, so in some ways, I thought that was the only way I could get attention. I was desperately searching for what I thought the father-son bond was supposed to be. I wanted the big "moment" I never had. I was searching for the I'm-proud-of-you-son moment that never came until my college graduation. I desired an acceptance that I saw with my friend's dads. This searching for acceptance was a trend that followed me until I was twenty-eight years old.

My father walked out on my mom when I was a baby, and my stepfather was the reason she had a mental breakdown and tried killing herself in February 2008. That's something I'll never forget, and it makes me thankful I was there to stop her. I guess in a lot of ways, we both wanted that acceptance that never came. My stepfather left me with black eyes, bruised legs, busted lips, and more. But more than anything else, he left me with trust issues, a broken mind, and a wound so big only God, intentional work, and therapy could heal it.

Eventually, just before my sixteenth birthday, I moved to Oklahoma City to escape him and learn how to be a teenager. I thought I had won since the events leading up to me moving were a fight and me literally threatening his life. What I didn't know is how much this was going to be an intentional effort on my part to learn to proactively deal with my issues and accept them as well. There were as many bad habits as there was trauma embedded in my life as a whole. It led to trust issues, bad relationships, drug use, a drinking problem, and even a near loss of my faith.

By the time I graduated for the second time in 2016, I had no identity except being who I thought people around me wanted me to be. I literally had no idea who I was or what I was pursuing. All I knew was that I wanted to get there fast. I was attempting to operate my own personal training business since that was what my degree was in, and I was also an associate pastor at a local church—two things I was not qualified to do, and I knew it while

I was working both of those jobs. I was not in the right state of mind to be in either of those positions. While running my business, I desperately sought the attention of the men I was in business with and the pastor I was working under in ministry. I sought their attention so bad that I changed nearly every detail about myself so that they would be proud of me. I changed my look, way of speaking, style of preaching, and even how I trained clients, just so I could hear, I'm proud of you, son. But it never came. I lost every client I had, and eventually, I lost my job as an associate pastor. The two things I wanted most, I lost within ninety days of each other, simply because I was looking forward instead of upward for approval.

My search for approval has taken me across the world, literally. It caused me to take jobs and move places I knew I never needed to go. I often went because I couldn't let go of my desperation to be wanted and the undying loyalty I had to those who cared nothing about my well-being or even if I wanted to be in the places I followed them to. As a matter of fact, they all dropped me the moment they were done with me. And that led me to a deeper, darker pit of lack and emptiness. My business suffered due to the choices I began to make, and I could never take the leaps I desired because I was too busy still following the plans of the people I followed over the God I should follow. I didn't even take myself seriously as a businessman until July 2021, after making entrepreneur endeavors for six years.

These choices, this longing for acceptance, were so detrimental that those things could have stopped my marriage before it ever had a chance to begin. I wanted this empty void to be filled so badly. I didn't realize the purpose God lovingly gave me was what would fill it. My most recent adventure led me to such a low point that I had no other choice but to admit I had no idea what I was doing and seek God and therapy to begin my healing journey.

This may sound crazy, but Nipsey Hussle and Snoop Dogg taught me the two best lessons about growth and business I could have ever learned. First, not everyone can join what you want to do in business and in life. Second, if they aren't willing to encourage you to grow, as well as grow with you, they absolutely have to go. Their acceptance isn't valid nor needed. This was a tough lesson to learn and an even harder habit to put into practice. Because in many ways, I am still that ten-year-old boy who wants to hear dad say, I'm proud of you, son. I'm still the boy who at age eight, asked his mom, "How come my dad doesn't want me?" I'm still him, and I always will be. The only difference is that now I constantly tell him that he is not the mistake of the fathers who could not play their role. I tell him that he is God's image and unconditional love personified and has the unique opportunity to share and introduce other young men to that love.

That's the thing about this journey I'm on—it's always going. There is no one-step cure-all. But the journey cannot begin until we begin looking upward instead of forward. Healing begins with acceptance, acceptance begins with acknowledgment, and acknowledgment begins with admitting that you have no idea what you're doing. That is when healing becomes a reality.

Dinetra Alford, CEO

Business: Brown Sugar Creations & LIFE Coaching
Website: http://www.twitter.com/itsniitraluv
Mission: Brown Sugar Creations: My mission is to bring joy to others by making personalized items for any occasion. LIFE Coaching: LIFE Coaching is dedicated to helping those seeking to find their passion and purpose. LIFE Coaching's goal is to improve relationships, boost confidence, and help push past the feeling of being stuck.

Bio: Dinetra Alford is a certified life coach. She is a lifelong helper and giver to those in need. Dinetra found her passion for helping others at a very young age and has used that passion to help others as a LIFE Coach. She also has channeled her creativity and started Brown Sugar Creations, where she provides customized items to customers.

Growing up, I always knew I wanted to be a helper. In grade school at parent-teacher conferences, my teacher would say things like She's always helping others; I was even voted most helpful in my class. I was so confident in those years and believed that I would really make a difference and did not question my abilities. However, being compared to my other siblings at home and teased for being smart at school, I began to compare myself to others and "dumb myself down" to fit in properly in school. Doing that did not make me feel better. I grew insecure in who I was; my self-esteem and confidence took a major hit. I felt that I did not fit in anywhere. I felt rejected and was rejected in many attempts to build a relationship, both platonic and romantic. The fear of rejection and wanting people's approval began to rule my life. I internalized every critique and criticism as a reflection of myself and tried to change who I was to be who I thought others wanted me to be.

Fast forward to adulthood. I have now decided to become a life coach to help others not experience the turmoil of healing alone and get through the fear of rejection, low self-esteem, and lack of confidence. I wanted to help others be free, so I started LIFE Coaching while continuing my education to become a licensed counselor. The problem was that I never truly got over my own fear of rejection and seeking others' approval at the time of starting LIFE Coaching, so I ran from my dream and left my business where I started it. I channeled my desire to make others happy into creativity and started Brown Sugar Creations. What started as a hobby became a passion. Seeing the look on others' faces when receiving a customized gift or seeing their idea come to life gave me the same satisfaction as talking others through their various problems. My passion is to truly help others. I did not feel qualified to be a life coach, for how can I coach someone else to wellness and wholeness when I felt like an impostor myself? It was impostor syndrome that kept me from going full throttle into LIFE Coaching like I desired. The feelings of inadequacy, the constant replays of childhood and adolescent criticism, opinions saying I am not good enough, not qualified, and being just flat out overlooked made me question if I could truly help and impact others. The fear of failure, the fear of success, as oxymoronic as it sounds, plagued me. How dare I try to help others when I am internally a disaster?

One night on a drive, feeling overwhelmed with feelings of under-accomplishment and wondering where I went so wrong in life and why I could only go so far, I cried and begged and pleaded with God to free me. He reminded me of Joshua 1:9 and his command to "be strong and courageous." As I rehearsed this Scripture and others like it, I began to feel my confidence rise, and the fear of what others think and the fear of rejection did not plague me as strongly as before. Yes, I still struggle with the fear of rejection and the approval of others, but it doesn't run my life and my business as much as before. I am not afraid to post my creations and customizations with Brown Sugar Creations anymore or tell people I do customizations. I stopped lowering my prices because I felt that's what people wanted and was afraid, they wouldn't purchase my product. I no longer hesitate when accepting orders from potential customers. I now work on ways to expand my offerings and improve on my craft. I began to plan how to relaunch LIFE Coaching and services provided ways to be consistent instead of hiding behind my fears and insecurities.

I've learned that it is important to focus on progress in this journey of healing and not how far you have left to go. I have learned to identify triggers, and instead of internalizing criticism as much as before, I do as my pastor says, "Eat the meat and spit out the bones." I started LIFE Coaching in 2017 and Brown Sugar Creations in 2020 and was so afraid to promote my businesses out of fear that no one would support my business, that I would mess up, that I would fail, that people would think I thought I was better than them. But I failed because I did not give myself a chance to succeed. Now that I have released my fear and insecurity, I have gotten more consistent business with Brown Sugar Creations and inquiries of when I will begin my coaching services with LIFE Coaching. I no longer overwork myself trying to please everyone, but now I have a balance. Healing has helped me set boundaries in all of my relationships and in my business, where I am no longer afraid or ashamed to be a business owner and make better decisions regarding my businesses and the clients I serve and will potentially serve.

Emerald Mills, Founder & President

Business: Diverse Dining
Website: www.4diversedining.com
Mission: Build Equity through Food and Dialogue

Bio: Emerald Mills is an author, business strategist, and the founder of Diverse Dining, an events/education organization that focuses on building equity through food and dialogue. Emerald founded Diverse Dining in response to a societal need to address racism and segregation and establish and maintain cross-marginal and cross-cultural relationships. The organization's unique approach to connecting people of all walks of life has been featured on a variety of news outlets including OnMilwaukee, Spectrum 1, Fox 6, The Milwaukee Journal Sentinel, VISIT Milwaukee, and various podcasts. In addition to serving as the founder and lead facilitator of Diverse Dining, Emerald recently published a book called Rejection Uprooted: 5 Practical Principles for Overcoming Rejection. In it, she shares her raw and uncut experiences with rejection and how she used her experiences as fuel to launch her organization.

I suffered from rejection and many of the other identified wounds throughout my life.

Of them all, rejection has been the most challenging to identify, address, and heal. The wound of rejection attaches itself to our identities. If not careful we can lose our sense of self and struggle with acceptance and belonging.

I believe that we spend most of our lives as humans trying to fit in or find a place of belonging. Our society has so many labels, identities, and classes. We are labeled for the foods we eat, the places we live, the color of our skin, our income, etc. Since the beginning of time, this strategy has been used to control and divide people. When we are rejected by individuals or by groups where we seek acceptance, our identity comes into question. We begin to ask ourselves questions like Who am I? What is wrong with me? Where do I belong? Why can't I just be like them?

If our parents or families reject us, or we have not developed a strong sense of self early on, all our future encounters can be affected. Often we become imbalanced in our need for acceptance. We either convince ourselves that we don't need or desire acceptance and, therefore reject others, or we compromise ourselves completely by forsaking all principles and values to gain the acceptance we seek.

By the time I started my career, I had developed the attitude that I really didn't need the approval or acceptance of others. I armored myself with many of the common beliefs like I don't come to work for friends, and you don't have to like me or agree with me for us to work together. Although these beliefs hold some truth to them, they positioned me on the inside of my own wall. In all honesty, this thinking did protect me from racism in my workplace, which still exists in many companies. I was also able to focus on the overall goal and why I was hired and not what people said or attempted to do to trigger me.

I found myself trapped in a self-imposed prison. I did not have any true accountability relationships because I did not trust people or myself. I sabotaged and cut off relationships before they got too close to me. Many of my decisions were based on the opinions of others and not what made sense to me.

I anticipated rejection and always stayed ten steps ahead of it. I became so masterful at this skill that I unknowingly took on the identity of rejection (I became it) in every place, every conversation, and every relationship. I talk more about that experience in my recently published book Rejection Uprooted: 5 Practical Principals for Overcoming Rejection.

Rejection affected my identity until it became my identity. I convinced myself that I did not need to be accepted and that I could still thrive without belonging or having the support of those around me.

This belief that I spent so much of my life operating under was a lie. I did desire acceptance, appreciation, and approval. Acceptance is a valid, basic need that every one of us holds. Our unexpressed needs do not simply go away.

I loved the work that I was able to do at my job; however, the environment that I worked in was toxic. I noticed about a year and a half in that the expectations placed on me by my employer were not realistic. I had received national recognition for my work and innovation. I was even being asked to participate in statewide committees and meetings. However, the organization for which I worked always found something wrong. I had no one to model my work after or to go to for guidance.

I tried to focus on the perks and benefits and pretend that the opposition didn't matter, but it did. In fact, because of all the other unhealed roots of rejection, it was magnified. I so wanted a healthy work environment that I made many adjustments to my work style.

The stress became so overwhelming that I signed up for therapy. I talked through various scenarios with my therapist, hoping that she would give me a strategy to make the stress go away and make me feel more empowered. Instead, she challenged me to think about why I wanted to stay. During my fourth session, my therapist made this statement: "Emerald, usually when people come here, they come because they want me to help them find their voice, but it seems like you want me to help you silence yours." She reiterated the statement by then asking me if that was what I wanted.

At that moment I knew I needed to make some adjustments, and I was no longer willing to compromise on my principles and values. I wanted and needed to find a place where I could be seen, heard, and valued. A healthy place where I could show up as myself fully.

Since I decided that my current work environment no longer served me, I started to reflect on my next move. As a mid-level career woman, my professional and financial expectations were high. However, as a caretaker of three children, I also needed an opportunity with enough flexibility to allow me to be present in their lives. Most importantly, I wanted my daily work to be meaningful and something I was passionate about—surrounded by people who embraced me.

I searched for and applied for several positions, but none of them met my full criteria. Deep down I always knew I wanted to be an entrepreneur. I spent over fifteen years signing up for class after class, cohort after cohort, various trainings, and seminars on entrepreneurship. I had more than enough education and information; however, feelings of inadequacy rooted in rejection always kept me from getting started. But this time I was ready to face my fears, embrace my talents, and bet on myself.

All entrepreneurs will face some level of rejection. I believe it comes along with the territory, especially when you are creating something never seen before. You will receive countless noes; however, my experience has taught me that the hardest no you'll ever encounter is the one that comes from you. So, often, the inner no (rejection) is derived from the limitations we place on ourselves, such as feeling unqualified, unprepared, or inadequate.

I was able to finish my business plan by getting really clear about my values and mission. I decided that my business would create the space I couldn't find for myself. I realized that I was not the only one who experienced this level of rejection. I decided to share my struggling and use it as a basis to create communities of acceptance.

My courage to face my fear of rejection has led to personal freedom. Not only have I obtained the things I desired in a career, but I now create safe spaces for others to show up authentically.

I would be lying if I said that my healing journey was easy. I was so comfortable in rejection that initially my healing was painful. However, living in true freedom is worth the pain, and it will ultimately unlock so many doors for your personal life and business.

Felicia Lee, Independent Consultant

Business: Felicia Michelle Jewelry
Website: www.feliciamichellejewelry.com
Mission: To bring independence, confidence, empowerment, and financial freedom.

Bio: Felicia Michelle Lee was born in Los Angeles, California, to Robert and Mary Lee. She is in the health industry and provides customer service to patients. As a Paparazzi Independent Consultant who has access to hundreds of $5 accessories, her pleasure is to create independence and an inheritance for business partners who join her team of six. In her not-so-spare time, she enjoys her ten nieces and nephews, going to the beach, and advocating for youth and seniors.

The words You were adopted had an impact on my life.

I didn't realize how those words would affect my life and at times bring up feelings of rejection. I am grateful for my parents and spiritual leaders who pushed me into fulfilling my destiny, which is still being written. It was easy for me to feel offended and have a tendency to push people away. The church was the first place that I had to work with other personalities. I know the Bible mentions that in this life, we will suffer, but I do not always comprehend what that looks like. The race is not given to the swift or the strong, but to the one who endures to the end.

Rejection is only a temporary nightmare. I have to learn daily in business and professionally that no man or woman is an island. Deadlines exist everywhere and are dependent on how well I work with others. One of my weaknesses is trusting that my peers will work together to meet a common goal. My experience had been that others tend to let deadlines fall through the cracks. Communication is a big deal in my opinion, which is why it was important for me to have a communications certificate. I have learned to communicate the needs with all levels of leadership, from the president to my peers. I believe in sowing and reaping the outcome.

Ethics and consistency play a big part in how others see you. People may never say anything to you, but I promise you, you are being watched. A big part of my life is to really let my word be my bond. Experiencing the feeling of rejection also helps me not want anyone else to feel the same thing. My body actions could turn off a potential customer or client. If folks believe I support others, it's because I have had people tell me what they would do for me, but it did not happen. I want my business to be supported, because I am genuine. People want to be a part of your life, and I have learned to include a piece of myself to connect.

In 2017, I started a new business with Paparazzi Accessories. I told myself, Felicia, Don't start another business where your success was dependent on others. I wanted to be successful on my own. Rule #1: Business doesn't work without other people. This statement is greater than the compensation. My mind had to start being in the business to help others. This is what I had missed during other business ventures. One must be customer service-oriented and care about others. Take things with a grain of salt and keep it moving. I take pleasure in seeing the face of my customers when I walk into a room with a jewelry bag.

Helping business partners see the vision for their lives and be successful has made me rich. Because I have experienced rejection, I can help them overcome and do a social media live. Rejection is a part of any business, and it builds character. Failure is not an option, and there are no off days.

Having good content is big within the social media world. In February 2018, I did my first Facebook Live, which did not have a lot of viewers. I told my team that people buy into you and want the authentic you. Hearing comments like You've come a long way or Wow, I didn't know you had that in you reminds me that being an overcomer is by deed only. I know I have a good product that is marketable and can change lives. Thankfully, growing a business is not the same as starting.

Jennifer Mattson, Fortune 100 Legal Executive

Business: Loving Mom, Wife, and Fortune 100 Legal Executive
Website: linkedin.com – Jennifer Maattson
Mission: Continuing to heal my soul on a journey to discard the lies I have believed, becoming my true self, and utilizing my journey to connect with others bringing His healing to a world in pain.

Bio: Jennifer Mattson is a legal executive who has worked for trade associations, financial institutions, payment and e-commerce companies, and the government. She has a passion for leading teams with servant leadership infusing grace back into the workplace and assisting people in finding their true selves and passions. She earned her Bachelor of Arts in Political Science from Gustavus Adolphus College and her Juris Doctorate from the William Mitchell College of Law (now Mitchell-Hamline), both in Minnesota. Jen, her husband Luke, and their three children, Masekela, Monte, and Ja'Ceon can be found hiking or biking through the great Metro, State, and National Parks most weekends. They recently added an RV (lovingly named Marge) to the family so they can explore more of the US and Canada.

My leadership skills first formed out of damage but ultimately were righteously restored through His truth revealed to me through healing.

Let me start at the beginning. My first abuse was at the early age of three. I was abused for many years thereafter during my childhood—sexually, emotionally, physically, and spiritually. That abuse caused a lot of pain, fear, damage, and hurt. I knew that I did not want anyone to see that damage, and I did not want to acknowledge the pain it caused me. I did not believe my abuse was something people wanted to deal with, and truthfully, I wanted to protect myself from what others would think of me, what I thought about myself, and sadly what I believed God thought of me.

So I made it my job to protect everyone, mainly myself and foolishly God—from my ugly truth. I did this by achieving and creating a hedge of perfection around myself. I commanded every moment of my life. Because when you are perfect, nobody looks close enough to ask questions. When you are perfect, everybody assumes you are doing great. So I used perfection as a shield to keep people away.

Because of this perfection—I was the one you wanted to have on your class project because I would make sure that my team got an A, and I would do all of the work to ensure that A. That made me feel good because I knew I was not going to let my guard down, and I was bringing people along with me, which at the time, I thought was successful leadership.

I also used humor and sarcasm, which I still use today—but as a child, I used these so people felt that they knew me. It feels inviting. It feels like you are getting to know me and getting closer to me. But really what I was doing was letting people in as far as I was willing, as far as I was comfortable. Are you noticing a theme of control yet?

I used these tactics—perfection, achievement, control, humor, and sarcasm—for many years and I was successful. Not only did I keep people from my ugly truth, but these tactics propelled me through school, sports, jobs, relationships, and faith (or so I thought).

But then these tactics, mainly perfection, became a weight that I carried around my shoulders, and in my last year of law school, I finally realized that it was killing me. I couldn't do it anymore. Through the intervention of the Holy Spirit, who utilized my mother at a lunch to lovingly ask me how I truly was doing—I finally put my hand up and said, "I need help."

My mother helped me find a Christian counselor who used what was then referred to as Theophostic Counseling (prayer-centered - Holy Spirit led healing). In that counseling, I was able to do many things. I forgave my abusers. I forgave those who turned a blind eye or did not notice my abuse. I forgave God for allowing free will which allowed my abusers the ability to hurt me (which I felt was God's abandonment of me). And I was able to forgive myself for the guilt I carried, for the belief that I deserved the abuse, all the decisions I made based on that abuse—including the pain I caused myself trying to be perfect, and all the opportunities I missed because I would not go after an opportunity unless I knew that I could succeed.

God provided me with the realization that the Dark Jealous (the name my daughter gave the devil when she was three) had used my abuse to twist my God-given talents and the desires of my heart. And with this realization and my surrender to His will, God restored in me my purpose and took these talents— the drive, the desire to achieve, and my personality (sarcasm and all) and restored them for His purpose. Through this healing, I put down the shame, take off the perfection, and relinquish the need to hide and truly receive His grace for the first time.

And with this restoration, God corrected my previous beliefs about leadership. I now know I do not need to be perfect. I do not need to be the one with all of the answers. I do not need to carry my team to success. All of my previous thoughts on leadership were about getting results. Instead, I learned I need to rely on God, replenish His gift of grace every morning, and lead my teams from the overflow. And by leading with His grace, I put people first and results second.

I also can lead with humility knowing what people present may not be the whole truth. I understand that the outside of what someone is giving you is not always what is going on underneath. Because every one of us has a story, all of us have gone through something that we are either trying to hide, survive, or have come out on the other side and are now using as a tool.

So, now knowing that it is not results that matter most in leadership but the grace you show people and the encouragement it provides, I strongly believe in and practice servant leadership. Not just the kind of servant leadership where you get in the mud with your team and show you will do the things you are asking them to do, but the kind of servant leadership where you show vulnerability. In this servant leadership, I lay myself down and share the things I did not do right in my life—personally or in my career. I share the ways I was able to overcome. I even admit to ways I am currently messing up and need their help. And by creating this vulnerability, there is a trust that forms. People begin to understand the environment that has been created and may share their vulnerabilities with you—allowing you access to pieces of themselves they may not otherwise share.

Through this grace-filled environment, people understand they can have fast fails allowing an agile work environment. People can go for those stretch opportunities because if it doesn't work out, we have this environment of trust and grace that we continue to go back to without shame. Through God's healing and example, I have created a leadership style opposite of my damage, allowing my teams the overflow of grace I never allowed myself. And to my younger self's surprise, in this place, there is a greater, more fulfilling success.

Lashondra Scott, President

Business: Neo Soul Productions
Website: neosoulproductions.com
Mission: To create superior imagery and strategic video solutions on multimedia platforms by translating visions into exceptional, compelling video that deliver measurable results.

Bio: Lashonda Scott is a visionary leader on a mission to change the conditions, mindsets, and attitudes of community residents through transformative and mission-driven films, television shows and new media. At an early age, Lashondra saw her life through the lens of a camera. She was 16 when she decided that television/video production would be her vocation. With that in mind, she attended Milwaukee Area Technical College (MATC) and earned an Associate's Degree in Television/Video Production. She then earned a Bachelor of Arts Degree in Business Administration from Cardinal Stritch University in Glendale, WI.

It all started after my fifth-grade graduation.

The day came when I was finally going to get out of elementary school, and I was excited to graduate from the fifth grade and go to middle school. I was ready to explore the next stage of my life, and I wanted to share my first graduation with my family. I got dressed and ran downstairs and asked my mom was she coming. She seemed kind of sad. I told her my teacher said parents could ride the bus home with their kids. She said, "I will try and make it." I never knew our financial situation; I just knew we always had a roof over our head, up-to-date clothes, shoes, and food on the table. We didn't have a car, but we always had a ride when we needed it. I remember additional people always lived with us because my mom didn't want any of our family on the street. So, if they needed a place to stay, guess what. It was with us.

That day, I walked out of the house hoping to see everybody cheering me on as I walked across the stage. I went on with my day, and I had a good morning at school. We had a half-day because our graduation program was at 1 PM. We came into the gym, and I looked to see if I could see any of my family, even if it was just my mom. I didn't see anyone. I thought, Maybe they are just late. As the program went on and we got ready to walk across the stage, I looked out in the audience, and I didn't see anyone.

My friend asked me where my family was, and I said, "I don't know."

My friend said, "You can celebrate with us and my mom will take you home."

I said, "No, I can't go because my mom won't know where I am." I was sad on the inside but appeared happy on the outside.

So, when I made it home, I asked my mom why she didn't come. She said, "I didn't have any money." Sometimes you tell yourself to be strong and move on to the next thing. This was the truth I told myself when no one showed up for me at my fifth-grade graduation.

As a kid, I learned that I had to depend on myself and not others. It was a hard lesson, one that was based on reality but not in truth.

I remember preparing for an event that was close to my heart titled I Dare You to Heal. I created this event because I wanted people to heal from traumatic events that happened in their life. I wanted to create a space for them to bring the things they've been most wounded by and process them. My greatest heart desire in the work I do and in the work I've done is to see people healed so they can live out their lives to the fullest. When others hurt, I hurt. I believe that you don't have to live your life on pause, you can move beyond your pain, and you can use your pain to fuel your purpose.

In the middle of a passion-filled project with all of the ingredients for success—I was faced with a fifth-grade wound: no one from my family showed up. Was the event a success? I'd like to think so, but the pain of experiencing the reality of people not showing up was triggered again.

When no one celebrates you, it often causes you to neglect to celebrate yourself. A few milestones in my life that essentially have come and gone are:

- becoming a homeowner at twenty-three
- recognition as a "treasure" in my hometown (Milwaukee Treasures)
- screenwriter, television director, novelist, and showrunner (John Ridley celebrated my gift and talent in film and storytelling. He boasted on me as being self-made.)
- business growth from a single entrepreneur to employing twelve and rising as the CEO of my company
- started a nonprofit

Eighteen years in business—and I've never celebrated it.

Learning to Trust the Process

As a business owner, you cannot be alone on an island. Having the belief that you have to do everything yourself will lead to you thinking no one will do it as well as you can; it will cause you to be tired and stressed out, and you will never grow. The truth is that you can depend on others, and people can be trustworthy. Yes, sometimes they may let you down; but trust is a learning process. To grow those on my team, I've learned that I have to step away sometimes and just guide them. I get to be the one that shows up for them and celebrates them. You cannot expand a business if you are not willing to trust them to do the work.

Perhaps you struggle with thoughts and questions like Can they really do the work? Do I need to be there? Can I trust them? Will they run off with all my stuff? Can I trust them with a key to the office? All those will make the job you need to do as a team more challenging. In the beginning, it made it hard for me because I did not trust them to show up. The first thing I've learned is to pause, reflect, and celebrate myself. Next, I've learned to begin to trust those around me and not enter every situation like it is my fifth-grade graduation.

As a business owner you must have a vision. Do work that you care about and keep challenging yourself. Face your fears because everything you have ever wanted is sitting on the other side of fear. Manage your energy because energy limits what you can do with your time. Don't be afraid to invest time in your company. Set goals and remind yourself of them each day. Remember that a goal without a deadline is a dream. Success only comes through action.

When it's time to hire, hire for character and values because you can always train someone on how to do a job, but you can't make someone's character or values fit your company after you hire them. If they align with your character and values, this will help you with your trust issues. Three ways you can build trust with your employees:

- Communicate, be true to your word, and follow through with your actions and promises.
- Be fair, honest, and admit to your mistakes.
- Support your team, get to know your team, and see the value in each team member. Don't just be their boss, be a mentor.

Last, know your customer and deliver more than is expected. It's a great way to get noticed in your industry and build a network of advocates.

Nancy Yarbrough, Founder & Executive Director

Business: Fresh Start Learning, Inc.
Website: www.freshstartlearninginc.org
Mission: We strengthen families, restore the underprivileged people of society, and rebuild communities. We are committed to advocating and raising awareness of social justice issues by strategically creating social development programs to transform the lives of those we serve and their environments.

Bio: Ms. Nancy Yarbrough is a social justice activist, victim advocate, author, public speaker, and the founder and CEO of Fresh Start Learning, Inc. I know firsthand that diminishing sex trafficking not only involves providing outreach and direct services to victims and survivors but also creating widespread community awareness of the reality of sex trafficking. I am currently a consultant, group facilitator-trainer working directly with victims to provide a realistic healthy healing journey.

I am the owner of Fresh Start Learning and the author of The Exodus—Where New Beginnings Happen. The business I founded came from discovering my purpose and passion through the pain I've experienced in my life. As my soul heals deeper, the growth I see in my business and my life is more profound.

One of the wounds that deeply impacted me is the wound of trust and unresolved issues.

I would find myself allowing things to happen in my life without addressing them. I took a passive posture: If I don't pick it, it won't bleed, or If I leave it alone, it will heal. Both thoughts were further from the truth. I've experienced various forms of abuse, from physical, verbal, sexual, emotional, and spiritual. I noticed that the abuse kept manifesting itself differently. It caused me not to trust and kept my heart in pain that I pushed past to try and perform as a business owner, mother, wife, and woman.

A profound wound that happened in my life and showed up in my business was spiritual incongruency from those I looked up to and admired. It sticks out to me the most because it triggered every other unresolved wound and issue in my life. I unassumingly believed that if a person in life or business presented themselves as a person of faith or as a Christian, I would not have to deal with some of the things I dealt with from people who made it clear they did not honor God. I did not expect them to honor me because I knew where they stood. When I encountered people of "faith" in marriage, business, and life who proclaimed to be men and women of God but whose actions were far from it, it was challenging for me to reconcile. Some would call this church hurt, but it extended to life and business hurt for me.

I recall the spiritual abuse I endured from my ex-husband. Its impact was the wound of trust as it reinforced all the unresolved issues and trauma from my previous life (learn more about this in my book The Exodus—Where New Beginnings Happen). At the time, I couldn't fully understand that this was a wound in how he would use God and the principles of marriage against me. It devalued the person I was; it made me feel less than what God had called me. My ex-husband's abuse manifested in many ways, and because he was a believer, I tried to do everything he told me to do. Even in all my efforts, I could never be good enough, saved enough, worthy enough for his love. I trusted the God in him, and I wanted to believe that he meant the best in his actions and behavior, but this was not true.

The pain of his disdain and degradation was bigger because, although I had experienced relational pain before, these were new waters. This person is supposed to love God; how could this be? I had never been with anyone who professed to be a believer, a man of God, and then experienced the pain I had known in the world. From the way he looked at me in the choir stand when my heart was truly to please God to the way his face frowned in my worship, I could not get it right. This scarred the very fiber of my spiritual soul. It was uncharted waters, and I had never been here before.

The one who was supposed to be the security for me was the one causing holes in my soul that only God would be able to heal and fill. Even when God delivered me from the situation, the residual effects were still there. I could feel the motion sickness from the turbulence of the relationship and the constant uncertainty it projected onto my identity. The unresolved issues were triggered, and they continued to come through every crack and wound I ever experienced. It continued to evolve and reinforced every lie I believed about myself. It made me question myself, and I began to wonder if there was a sign on my forehead that read "target for hurt and pain here." I carried the weight and burden of What did I do and how can I fix this?

The unresolved issues and wounds from this old marriage found their way into my business. I would find myself bringing all my gifts to the table in business. I would give everything I had. If someone professed to be a Christian, believer, or person of faith, I felt compelled to prove to them that I was worthy, that I was worth it. I went in open, the same way I did in the marriage. Again I met men and women who presented themselves as people of God and experienced the same behaviors manifesting against me. I was back trying to prove I was worth it. I was trying to prove I was just as important as they were and that my past didn't mean I wasn't called to do the work I do. I wanted them to know that God had given me a very specific gift and purpose to fulfill because of my past.

When people present themselves as being one way, I believe them. When things would go bad in the Christian collaborations, it would pick the wounds of unresolved issues and trust open again. My heart would bleed. I would feel discouraged and in a cycle of wanting to quit and walk away. Certain environments would make me feel like I didn't deserve to be at the table. When God began to heal my soul, He reminded me that He is the one who prepared the table.

I noticed that the courage He gave me to walk away from the spiritually abusive marriage was the same courage He would give me to recognize when a collaboration threatened my spiritual and emotional safety. I had permission to walk away then as well. I've had to walk away from unhealthy business connections that inflicted spiritual abuse and took advantage of the innocence of my unassuming nature. I believed that if we all love God, we will do the things that God loves. I learned that isn't always true. Learning this reality devastated me. Just like in my marriage, in business, it was uncharted waters to connect with people who would say they love God but would be undermining in business practices or would shade me because of my past and disregard my current impact.

It blew me away.

It required me to go back and heal the unresolved issues so that when I encountered these situations, I wouldn't be triggered and struggle so profoundly with trust. Many business owners still walk around with superficial wounds because of unmet expectations. Those who have genuine hearts and expectations encounter others who are still on their healing journeys, and their behaviors reflect that. Complete healing in this area for me is coming from God. Coming as He reminds me of who I am and secures me in my identity that I am His. He approves me, and I don't have anything to prove to anyone else.

Wounds of unresolved issues and trust wounds can often cause impostor syndrome to become active in your life. You'll begin to question who God decreed you were before the beginning of time because of something someone who has no authority to speak over your future has said—healing your soul matters. My business is growing, and it continues to grow because I am healing, and I continue to heal. When I'm invited to sit at tables God has prepared, I don't look for the approval of those at the table. It doesn't matter to me if they present themselves as a faith-filled business owner or a secular business owner. What matters to me the most now is my awareness of who I am. What they say or do doesn't change that.

If you find yourself questioning who you are, changing who you are, or hating who you are in business or life, I encourage you to ask God to show you who you are. Ask Him to secure His truth in your soul in a way that no one else can change or shake it. If you want to learn more about my life, journey, and my exodus, please reach out to me at nancy-theexodus.com or www.freshstartlearninginc.org.

Sandra Oliver, Owner & Operator

Business: Ordinary World Photography
Website: Ordinary World Photography – Facebook
Mission: To capture and share God's amazing grace through photography as a means of offering hope, peace, and understanding of God's creations.

Bio: I am a licensed clinical social worker by day and a photographer by mandate. I have been capturing God's creations for twelve years, and my ultimate goal is to travel the world photographing as much as God allows me to see and share His majesty, grace, beauty, and creativity with the world. Photography doesn't necessarily need a description. The images speak for themselves and leave no question as to what is.

Wounds of Rejection— this wound may manifest as the man alone on an island, not going after a business idea or goal because of perceived or actual rejection and shame.

Wounds of rejection often run deeper than one can imagine. Rejection comes in many areas of life, from childhood to the present day. For myself, rejection caused me not to trust anyone, not believe in myself, and not feel worthy enough to dream of owning a business. As the years went by, healing of my soul occurred, and the dream began to take shape—the vision and desire to own my own photography business. The dream continues to grow! I have worked the past three to four years diligently honing my skills, learning about business practices, and creating an inventory from which every imaginable product can be created using my photographs.

I didn't trust anyone to support me in my dreams as I had been put down for dreaming throughout my life. I didn't trust anyone to not steal my ideas (as if), and I didn't trust myself to follow through on my dreams of owning a photography business. In fact, there have been many instances of self-sabotage over the years, especially when it came close to being successful with projects. As a mental health therapist, I work with people day in and day out who deal with many fears, one of the biggest being rejection. Out of fear of rejection, I didn't speak about my photography and the private thoughts I had about owning a business for many years. I knew better!

I chose to heal the deep soul wounds I had carried with me since childhood and to denounce the lies I believed. I told myself lies daily, and the biggest lie of all is God doesn't love me or care about me. He doesn't hear me. Finally, choosing to think, believe, and react differently to life and healing the past, shifting my thoughts, and building a personal relationship with God has allowed me to believe that I am worthy of owning a business, dreaming abundantly, dreaming with excitement, and sharing a part of myself with the world.

I am hosting my first photo exhibit, open to the public with canvases on display and for sale. This took many hours of conversations with God, friends, believers, and myself to make this exhibit come to fruition. This is the real deal! Through God's provision, canvases, easels, the exhibit space, and everything else needed for the show has been obtained. I know without a glimmer of doubt that this show will be successful and will be a stepping stone to the next level. My dream of exclusively doing photography to make a living is even closer. New contacts have been and will be made, and new outlets and opportunities will arise, and more work will be created. Soon, I will be self-sufficient—well, not self-sufficient as God will always be a part of me and my business.

I have accepted that not everyone has to like or love my photographs, that everyone has different likes and dislikes and different tastes, and that beauty is subjective.

Because of my fear of rejection, I could not handle any type of criticism until I understood that criticism was not always detrimental and could in fact be positive. If someone didn't like my work, it didn't mean they didn't like me or that I had failed. That is a whole other ball of wax that had to be melted and reshaped! I know that my work is excellent and that God approves; he gave me the gift of photography seeing through his lens. His approval and understanding are all that I need to be successful—I am already successful. I don't have to be a millionaire to be considered successful; if I sell one photograph or canvas, I have succeeded. Getting up every day, thanking God for my blessings, being grateful for what I have, maintaining my personal relationship with God, and stopping the fear of rejection all make me successful.

Understanding these successes allows God to flow through me and into my work and allows me to share with the world God's amazing grace. All one needs to do is look at his creations captured in one millisecond, forever frozen in time, to understand that there is something or someone much greater than myself or ourselves maintaining this Earth. For myself, that is God; there can be no other.

Rejection is "the dismissing or refusing of a proposal, idea, offer, etc., the spurning of a person's affections, the dismissing of a person's feelings, emotions, needs, and wants" (Oxford Languages Dictionary). For many, rejection equals Nobody loves me, nobody cares, nobody supports me, I am doing this all by myself, I don't have anyone, and God doesn't love me. Every perceived slight becomes magnified, and a person loses themselves in self-pity, distrust, anger, guilt, shame, and fear of simply living life. It means that if one feels rejected, one will reject all others, including God, as a means of self-protection. It is how humans function; it is our nature until a personal relationship with God is built and maintained and until the soul is healed.

Sonia Adams, Founder & CEO

Business: I Am Pretty, LLC and Blossom Network
Website: iamprettycommunity.com / soniaadams.com / https://www.instagram.com/soniaaadams/
Mission: I Am Pretty, LLC, community helps garner relationships among young and mature women nationally and internationally. Within the community, we host transformative events in business, personal life, and beyond. The collaboration and networking happen organically, and we create space for women to express their vision and be supported spiritually and financially. Five key goals of the I Am Pretty community include: relevant content and conversations; connections and collaborations that enrich women; provides spiritual and educational resources to aid in personal development; opportunities to share your gifts, glean from other women, and garner financial resources; a safe space to share stories, experiences, and ideas. This LLC sells products displaying the I Am Pretty brand to young girls, teenagers, and women, and its goal is to empower women in their self-worth and embrace a brand that speaks to their internal and external pretty.

Bio: Sonia is a dynamic communicator and shares relevant perspectives in her writing, speaking, and business that empowers women. Her content and products affirm women's self-worth and identity. Sonia self-published three books. Her book I Am Pretty ignited the I Am Pretty brand, movement, and I Am Pretty, LLC. She received her BS from Tuskegee University and her MA in Theology from Oral Roberts University. Sonia is married to Shawn Adams with their sons, Solomon and Simeon Michael Adams.

Rejection is the nemesis that grabs the opportunity to puncture our hearts and damage our souls. It is ever-present and shows up when we least expect it. It strikes the core of who we really are and attempts to drain our strength so that we will not walk in our full purpose with power and confidence. An incident where I experienced rejection that caused my self-worth to hit rock bottom was when someone spoke disheartening words to me at a tender age. I was eager and ready to conquer the world, and I hurried to this person whom I esteemed highly and shared my life's dream— he told me I would never fulfill my dream because women are not equipped to do what I dreamed. I was told if I aspire to fulfill this dream, everything I touched would fail. It was that place in my life that rejection from a person I admired caused my identity to depreciate and spiral into a twenty-four-year journey to find value, worth, and confidence.

I did everything in my power to prove him wrong and earn his affirmation. However, the cycle to win his approval left me unsure and caught in a phase of trying to win his and others' approval. I was caught in a performance trap that drained me mentally, spiritually, and physically. This wound clouded my view and did not allow me the freedom to pursue my goals with joy or assurance.

Though I continued my path toward success, pessimistic thoughts triggered unhealthy behavior or responses as I chased my business dreams. As I pursued ministry as a pastoral leader, I spoke boldly, confronted justice, and challenged unhealthy practices and inequitable systems.

Consequently, there were times I received backlash because of my boldness. This backlash manifested in the form of people rejecting me. Other times, people distanced themselves from me, dissolved our relationship, or disappeared. These hurtful occurrences continued to rattle my confidence and shake my resolve. Even after attempts to bounce back, rejection continued to show up and deepen the wound in my heart. After utilizing my grit to continue my vision, I participated in a merger that did not work but quenched my creative flow. The leader rejected many of my ideas, excluded me and my strong personality as a Black female leader. I began to withdraw from some and felt intimidated by others. I became passive and paranoid about everything. Intimidation had taken root in my heart, and I lost my self-assurance and no longer felt purposeful or accepted. I entered a state of depression and spiraled into an abyss of self-loathing, rebellion, and worldly gratification to ease the pain and forget the hurt.

I needed God to do for me what I could not do for myself. I needed his touch to help me come out of that dark place and give me passion and purpose again. When I finally exhausted all my strength, God came in and rescued me. He gave me a rope and pulled me out of the abyss, and began to nourish me back to health.

How many times have others rejected you, but you bounced back amid adversity? How many times have you made a way out of no way and pressed your way to continue to survive because so many people depend on you? Although rejection scarred you mentally, physically, and spiritually, you keep going because something in you will not let you quit. Like me, if you do not get healed entirely, you may experience burnout or break down. Fortunately, healing is also available to you. Can you recall the time or that place where you were rejected, and it left you feeling empty, void of purpose, or trying to prove something to yourself and others to quiet the voices in your head of those who said you could not, would not, or never would be?

Additionally, this place can occasionally trigger things in your mind, cause doubt, and create a lack of belief in pursuing your dreams. Many times, our past holds us in bondage to our future. Rejection can show up when negative words are spoken to us, abuse happens, or love and support are absent at a vulnerable time in our life. Failure of a dream, relationship, or divorce can also cause rejection.

If we do not see ourselves whole and affirmed, the shame could cause us to become paralyzed and never reach our dream, and we may find ourselves sitting alone in sorrow. Therefore, deep work in your heart will aid in overcoming that place where you were rejected.

This process of healing will not happen overnight. It is a journey of believing, doubting, and failing. Within my journey, I achieved success; sometimes, I feel paranoia while stepping forward then backward, but I continue pressing toward God and his purposes for my life. Little by little, day by day, I have learned to forgive those who hurt me and let go of the resentful feelings. I've renewed my passion and gained new insight regarding the next phase of my purpose. I understand that the rejection I experienced was all a part of God's plan to teach me to trust Him wholeheartedly.

I also recognized that my self-worth was not in my performance. God uniquely created me with distinct peculiarities, a prophetic edge, a compassionate heart, and a boldness to speak up for others. I've determined to love everything about me unapologetically. I grasped that I was being prepared to do more excellent work and produce triple what I had built in the past. The disapproval of men no longer binds me, but I am free to follow God's purpose by yielding to Him continuously. The best is yet to come, and the vision is more significant than I could have imagined.

As you heal completely, you will also produce greater. Every disappointment and rejection is all a setup for success. You know exactly where you are in this season of your life, so be patient with yourself and with God. If you're willing to be vulnerable and visit places where you were rejected, receive God's affirmation, and journey through His process of healing, your healthy state of mind will produce profitable and lasting results in your business and your life.

Stacey Shaw-Virgo, President & Co-Founder

Business: Destined To Be Free
Website: destinedtobefree.org
Mission: Advocate for women in transition.

Bio: Stacey Dianne is a multifaceted, self-motivated individual with twenty-five plus years of C-level senior administrative office management experience for multifamily real estate development and multifamily construction. Her diverse background encompasses facilities management, business ownership, real estate support, and owning her own virtual assistant and business consulting company. Stacey is a licensed real estate agent in the state of Maryland and the president and co-founder of Destined To Be Free.

I have always desired to be seen, heard, and loved by my father. This has always been something I have held on to. Not receiving my father's love and approval the way I expected to receive it or wanted to receive it caused so much havoc in my life and my business. I wanted to please my dad; I wanted to receive the attention my brother receives; I wanted to receive my cousin's attention. I love you so much, daddy. Why can't you love me the way in which you love my brother and my cousin? Why can't you support anything I do? Why do you have to be so verbally abusive? Why can't you just be that dad who adores his daughter and would move heaven and earth for her? Well, he is not that type of person, and it wasn't until the past two years that I learned that all the wounds, pain, and hurt that I have been carrying around were partially due to the pain and hurt from my dad.

This affected every area of my life. I know I am called to the marketplace, but unless I took the time to do the work, where I began learning to heal, seeking God, finding out who I truly am, and begin making myself a priority, learning to set boundaries, I would only be called to the marketplace but I wouldn't be in the marketplace. Every business—and I mean every business—that I started failed. Nothing I did lasted more than three years. Why? My pain and hurt were showing up in my business. The way in which I would conduct myself, the way I operated my business, being a people pleaser, seeking validation, the need to always be praised, wanting to be loved by my clients, and not knowing the difference between friendship and business relationship created unhealthy relationships. I didn't know how to value myself and the work I did, so whenever a client wanted me to do work for them for free or for less than what I am worth, I would give in and do it, even though I knew I shouldn't.

My businesses suffered, my organization suffered. Even when I worked in corporate America, my jobs suffered. I didn't know what love was, and I covered up my pain.

It took having a meltdown due to being in an unhealthy relationship with someone where I was emotionally abused, which led me to realize I needed help. I couldn't continue the way I had been living. I had to learn how to turn around my life and business.

I began therapy, which worked for a while, but the one thing that really began to help me to shift and make changes in my life was when I decided to take a soul care practitioner certification with my mentor and coach. At first, the purpose of the certification was to help survivors leaving a domestic violence relationship, but as I began going through the lessons, I realized I was actually working on myself and that I was never healed, and I was still messed up.

To date, I am not totally healed, but I am not where I used to be. I had to make the decision that I was going to do the work. Some days I just didn't want to do anything, but if I didn't I would only be hurting myself. A few recommendations I would like to share with you if you find yourself in a situation similar to mine:

- Acknowledge that you may need help or you may need to make changes in your business. You may need to take a sabbatical.
- Learn to rest. Rest does not mean you are not doing anything; it means you lean into the Father and trust him and do what he tells you to do. Nothing more. Rest in him.
- Remove the term "hustle and grind" from your life if this is something you do.
- Set a time for work, a time for fun, a time for sleep.
- Make your health a priority, not just healthy eating, but including exercise, drinking your required amount of water.
- Seek God with everything you are doing in your personal life and business.
- Keep a journal, which could be a notebook or if you prefer to keep an electronic copy, you can use Google Docs. Type out your thoughts, plans, dreams, or anything the Holy Spirit shares with you.

- Have the right support system in every aspect of your life. Having a coach or a mentor is so important; having a team of like-minded people in your circle you can bounce off ideas with but more importantly, who will pray with you, encourage you, stand with you through the ups and downs, and even just hang out and laugh.
- Maintain your healing. Take the necessary steps to begin your healing process and do the work, whatever that may be. If you don't, there will be a relapse.
- Let go of all the pain, learn to forgive, set healthy boundaries, and walk in love.
- Find out what is needed to create or operate your business from the kingdom.
- Know what your calling is, know your gifts, know your numbers.
- Take the time to plan and do the necessary research required. Create a detailed and thorough structure. Create healthy processes, hire the right team, and never be afraid of delegating.
- Be authentic. Be you. Love yourself.
- Make your home your safe space.

Being able to walk in your true identity and being able to live a life of healing is so freeing. It helps to open doors you never thought would be opened. It allows you to walk in peace and joy. Trials will arise, setbacks may pop up, but once you decide to live the life you were created to live and impact the lives you were created to impact, you will do what is needed and required. I leave with you one of my favorite Scriptures, which I stand on— "I no longer call you servants, because a servant does not know his master's business. Instead, I have called you friends, for everything that I learned from my Father I have made known to you" (John 15:15 NIV).

Stephen Holder, Administrator

Business: Brothas Onsite
Website: Stephan Holder on Facebook
Mission: My goal is to tackle difficult social, political, and sometimes religious issues while creating a safe space and dialogue to vent our difference while seeking understanding of opposing viewpoints.

Bio: Stephen C. J. Holder grew up on the northwest side of Milwaukee, Wisconsin. He has been consistently practicing a life dedicated to Christ since age six. He attended Rufus King International Baccalaureate School for the College Bound, graduating in 2003. Following this, he attended Marquette University, receiving a bachelor's degree in communication studies with a minor in theology. He currently attends Christian Faith Fellowship Church in Racine, Wisconsin, serving as a men's Bible study teacher.

Let's play a game. Time yourself and see how fast you can answer this question.

Quickly . . . What is 1 + 1?

I am almost certain everyone reading this gave the same answer. I'd be willing to bet it was the first math problem you learned. What if I asked you, Can you prove to me that 1+1=2? I am certain most people would use the proverbial apple example. If you have one apple and add another apple, you have two. Well . . . yes, that is an illustration of how 1+1 is 2, but the real question is Can you guarantee me in every instance, this equation can hold as true? Is it possible to tell someone 1+1 will always be two? All of us were shown the apple illustration, and from that day, we said, Yep, that's how life works, but what if it didn't?

Just one time, what if this equation, this formula we trusted in so boldly, had an instance where it didn't work?

I grew up not only believing in this formula, but I also lived it, preached it, held it, cultivated it, and aspired to it, not realizing I carried more faith in the formula than faith in myself. I think we are taught early on to embrace life in formulas just like 1+1=2. I was told if you respect and treat others well, you would get it back in return. I was told that if you work hard in school and academics, you will be successful. If you went to college, you would be able to create a great life for yourself. If you held on to your virginity for the right woman, you would have a blessed marriage. If you showed diligence at your job, you would be appreciated, promoted, and revered. Life's formulas! If I had to put a spin on my own definition of rejection, I'd say, when someone has applied the formulas they have been taught, and they don't render the anticipated or expected outcome.

I grew up in a Pentecostal church (Church of God in Christ denomination). I truly was a poster child for the belief system because, in my mind, this was a means to please God—the only means—and in order to be right, I had to meet the approval of the leadership and God. From childhood to about twenty, this formula made sense to me until an interesting series of events took place. During my freshman year of college, I entered my first adult relationship. The person I dated used to go to church as a young child but drifted out, which was fine to me because she was more than willing to go to church with me. After a few months, she even joined my church. I truly believed this was meant to happen, and our relationship was meant to succeed.

Things were okay for the first six months of the relationship, but then things began to unravel. You see, I didn't grow up knowing about "game," so a lot of things took place on the side of manipulation and strategy on her part, and I had no clue. I just didn't know or understand it. We were always in situations where we were alone, and sex would always somehow craft its way into the scene as an option. I wanted to wait till marriage before entering that world, and though we had some close calls, we never had intercourse. I remember even telling my pastor about the near-fall situations, and he told fellow pastors and leaders, applauding me for leaving those situations. Honestly, I felt the sexual attention was flattering, but I strongly desired to enjoy it in marriage. The sexual invitations reached a very scary point. Hard to explain the one instance, but I'll try.

One day, I stopped by her house after classes, as I did most days before catching the number 57 bus to head home. Once again, she attempted to have intercourse. I said no and hoped to continue just enjoying the time together watching a movie, or having a nice talk before catching the bus to head home. This time was different than most. Before, it was just a flirty suggestion with a smidge of seduction, but this time was aggressive and demanding.

The room became dark and eerie. It was the look of a storm approaching outside, making the room very quiet and dim. I called her name to wake her from this bizarre trance she appeared to fall into. She said, "Stop calling me that," in a slightly altered voice from her normal tone.

At the same time, my mom was calling my old-school Kyocera Sprint analog cellphone urgently, but there was too much going on for me to answer. The phone had to ring about fifteen times total, in intervals of five rings, with a voicemail, pause, and callback.

My girlfriend (who wasn't answering to her name) said, "There is something in you that won't let me in. Why don't you just let me in?" and proceeded to unbutton her top. I knew this was purely supernatural, and it was time to leave. I attempted to walk out of the house, but she held onto my leg like a five-year-old, refusing to let go as I took each step from the upstairs common area to the front door.

Not too long after all this occurred, I ended the relationship. Things had become very frustrating, and it was clear they would not get any better. As a man, of course I wanted to have sex, but I wanted to please God and do it correctly. Once I realized we just weren't on the same page with the abstinence plan, I had to end it.

After the breakup, she stayed at the church and eventually became very close to the leadership. There was an attempt to get back together but to no avail.

Our church had our annual set-up meeting in January 2005 (four months after our second breakup). Many people showed up as we basically met to discuss and assign people to either new positions in the church or just to reaffirm people would continue in their old positions. I was the men's Sunday school teacher, being twenty at the time, which was odd and an honor because I was also the youngest person in the class. I remember the pastor going over the names of the people and their positions. In the middle of the meeting, he said, "Due to Brother Holder not living up to the criteria of the position, he will have to sit down and no longer teach any classes." I thought I misheard it. But before I could respond or think of anything to say, he continued. "We have been getting reports of you not living up to the standards for the position."

I reviewed it all in my head: I have never drunk alcohol; I don't cuss at all; I don't smoke anything, nor do I desire to be around it; I don't lie; I don't cheat, steal, play no card games other than Uno; and Lord knows, I wasn't having sex with anyone. I had no idea what he could be talking about. I held back tears the rest of the meeting, not sure what to think. Some people looked back at me with a snarly look as to say, See, I knew that goody-two-shoes thing was fake. Some of these are people I've known for years. I felt they knew me. I felt my integrity was beyond reproach, especially with the pastor, whom I viewed as a father figure. He taught me manhood things as well as church business. He taught me how to fix a tire, which screws and screwdrivers to use for which materials, how to paint, the proper way to lift heavy things. Surely, he would have come to me before assuming any misrepresentation?

That following Sunday, I wasted no time going to his office, asking him what happened and what I was being accused of. He couldn't look me in the eyes. He just looked down and said, "I was told you were having sex with your ex-girlfriend and still trying to teach the Sunday school class. We can't have that. What was I supposed to do?" My heart sank for quite a few reasons. I believed if someone showed themselves trustworthy, they would have an intact reputation. I believed if someone obeyed God's Word and leadership, they would be held beyond reproach. I believed 1+1 was 2.

I was so hurt I couldn't say much after that. I told him, "I haven't slept with anyone. As a man in my twenties, it's kind of odd to defend not sleeping with someone. But even if I was, why couldn't you come to me? Why couldn't you just ask me? I've never lied to you before." He didn't answer and abruptly got ready for the Sunday service.

Many years later, everyone discovered it was a lie spun by my ex, but the damage was already done. There was never a real I'm sorry, or We were wrong. I was able to give messages a few times after that, but I was still hurting. The closest thing to an apology from anyone was, "Well, you know there are three sides to every story." To this day, I still hate that phrase. I didn't know how to function in many capacities after that. I didn't question my relationship with God per se, but I did question my confidence in teaching or serving God in the capacity of church positions. This insecurity slowly crept into other things. It did make me question church culture. Where was the people's discernment? Where was the prophesying on my behalf?

Where was the person to stand on my integrity? Of course, my mom did and a few others, but as a whole, my confidence was gone. How do people shout and dance at church until they are red in the face (even if they are Black with dark skin) and be so off about my character? Why didn't anyone consult God about me? Surely if we all serve the same God, he would give everyone the same answer concerning me.

That was my first taste of the "new math"—the math the world truly operates in. To many people, church and salvation weren't about integrity but rather tithes, coming to anniversaries and conventions, and rubbing elbows with the right people. I saw people I knew were crooked being promoted to national positions, all because they spoke in tongues or performance and flattery. Even my ex-girlfriend ended up with a state church position. I watched the person who killed my reputation be elevated through the ranks. What was crazier was having friends and associates at our school showing me nasty messages she sent them to do "favors."

I became divided, knowing the teachings of Christ and his doctrine, yet seeing the practices of many churches. I was conflicted because all the things I was reading didn't match what I was taught. For example, I was taught you had to tarry for the Holy Spirit and speak in tongues to prove his presence, yet the Word says that once saved, the Holy Spirit is a gift (and gifts don't require tarrying). The only condition was to be holy for the Spirit to dwell. It also says that tongues were one of many manifestations of the Holy Spirit, but not exactly an indicator. The only indicator given in Scripture was the workings of the "fruit of the Spirit," which allows us to carry the personality of Christ, giving us a fighting chance to live holy in this world. This conflict led to some heated debates between me and many other people and leaders. Usually, it would end with them getting upset and me not having a liking for more church culture, but no resolution.

By 2013, I was a wreck. I left the church I grew up in to help out at a friend's church, where she left me in charge for a year while she visited her family in Texas. When the leader came back, we had some clashes on some doctrinal things as well. And I was completely fed up. I started visiting a church that I truly admired, but I knew it wouldn't be permanent.

It may sound crazy, but I was truly afraid to commit to a church home for fear of rejection. I feared giving my all in every capacity and being turned against for the slightest misunderstanding. I began to develop ideas of just not being good enough and not wanting to share my gifts with anyone. I love teaching, but I didn't want anyone to know I could teach. I love leading discussions, but I didn't want to establish relationships with anyone. I love writing, but I fell into a slump where all I could write about was failures and my new scope of myself: failing the formula. Part of me was burning to exhibit my gifts, to speak hope into people's lives, but all I kept playing in the back of my head was that set-up meeting and being denounced in front of all those people. I couldn't afford to relive that again.

My mom saw the frustration I was going through and asked if she could read a book to me. Odd, considering I am grown, and I can read very well on my own, but she said the book can only really take shape if I just listen rather than reading, so I did. She read me The Shack by William Paul Young. Not to give away the book at all, but it portrayed God in a way I had always hoped, always desired, but never thought possible due to my teachings and indoctrination. It showed how God loves us so much and how we turned him into a formula, which limits our love experience.

The pressures and expectations to make attendance at convocations, the hell and doom of not paying tithes, our distaste for certain sins isn't even how God functions. Through Christ, who the Son sets free is truly free indeed, and in love, though there are standards and holiness, serving God is not on the condition that my experience on the planet be more pleasant or fulfilling based on deeds or the approval of others. It's about the relationship. He wants to know me. He desires to know my fears, hurts, stresses, and joys, and his relationship isn't held hostage to rubbing the right elbows with the right figures.

When you love Him, you seek the things he is about freely. The idea of church is huge and important to Christ, for he is married to the church and it is a living body, but you can't lose sight of the people while protecting the sanctity of the building. The world is not always us versus them, but rather seeking compassion and to live peaceably among all men if it is possible. The truth was, even if I did have sex with my ex, God didn't love me any less. If my record wasn't perfect, his love was not on the condition of my attributes. He wasn't even keeping score. He wasn't keeping tally. He loved

Stephen as Stephen. The issue was never him loving me; it was loving myself if I didn't match up to the attributes.

I still have never drunk, yet the diagnosis is still out on if I have a liver issue at this very moment. I have never smoked, but my lungs were still a problem. I didn't have intercourse until my marriage; I still had a divorce. Tried to be as healthy as possible; still gained a ton of weight. Did well in school and got a good degree; still struggled to get a good job. The true test of self-love is, can I love Stephen when 1+1 doesn't equate to 2? Could I break free from both the formulas I was taught and the formulas I entrapped myself in?

Love, like salvation, is a choice you make every day. You determine how you will protect yourself through the day, how you will carry your esteem, who you let in your circle, and how you will conduct yourself if things don't go right. Love is a choice, and you have to choose yourself every day. Many of the journeys set before us were not by choice, but you can choose the esteem and attitude you carry during the journey. There are people born with missing limbs while having two healthy parents. Some faithful women got HIV from husbands they treated like kings. Some people lost jobs they were never late to or called in sick for. The question is, can you serve God when the formula didn't work?

After my mom read me the book, I saw the issue was in loving me more, and the more I grew to love myself, the more I could benefit others and live in the freedom to share my gifts to honor God without fear. Ironically, it would be another four years until I fully grasped this new concept of freedom. My new love for myself allowed me to find a church home with a pastor who understood this freedom and loves people the way I grew to understand love. My new love for myself allowed me to recognize that I was in an emotionally abusive marriage and leave right away without fear of the divorce stigma. Understanding even in divorcing, there is a way to honor God and love correctly. I also began sharing this new concept of love via social media, which led to being asked to speak on shows and panels. I currently have a Facebook page titled Brothas OnSite, where I along with some college friends discuss hard social issues that divide most people. We try to find not just common ground but provide a space for people just to express their hurts, insecurities, and frustrations with opposition.

Saved or not, we all share a planet, and I want the light and love God has given me to shine and touch those who feel trapped in the formulas they forced themselves into. Jesus's entire life was 1+1, not even being close to equating to 2, and he spent his entire ministry encouraging others to love themselves and seek his ways in order to love themselves and each other. The church and the world sometimes have it mixed up a bit. God didn't make rules for himself, because he needs no order nor discipline; rather, he made rules for us because he knows we are predisposed to hurting ourselves due to our selfish and sinful nature, and his perfect will is that we prosper even as our souls prosper. His holiness is to engulf and permeate our souls so we can live our best lives, without the fear of 1+1 not being 2.

REFERENCES

Allendar, Dan B. (2000). The healing path: How the hurts in your past can lead you to a more abundant life. WaterBrook Press.

Backus, William & Chapian, Marie. (2000). Telling yourself the truth: Find your way out of depression, anxiety, fear, anger and other common problems by applying the principles of misbelief therapy. Bethany House Publishers.

Bradshaw, John. (1990). Homecoming: Reclaiming and championing your inner child. Bantam Books.

Calhoun, Adele Ahlberg. (2015). Spiritual disciplines handbook: Practices that transform us. IVP Books.

Capacchione, Lucia. (1991). Recovery of your inner child: The highly acclaimed method for liberating your inner self. Simon & Schuster/Fireside.

Crabb, Larry. (2001). Shattered dreams: God's unexpected path to joy. WaterBrook Press.

Keller, Timothy. (2015). Walking with God through pain and suffering. What is grief and why does God allow suffering? Penguin Books.

Mayers, Marvin K. (1987). Christianity confronts culture: A strategy for cross cultural evangelism. Zondervan.

Passini, Daniel. (2017, October 30). The father wound: What it is, its effects, and how to heal. Dr. Daniel Passini. https://danielpassini.org/father-wound/ .

Porat, Shawn. (2017, July 7). Why trust is a critical success factor for businesses today. Forbes. https://www.forbes.com/sites/theyec/2017/07/07/why-trust-is-a-critical-success-factor-for-businesses-today/?sh=2b254765df0c

Sinclair, Lisa. (2020). Restoring the paths: Sexuality for Christian leaders. T.A.L.K. Publishing, LLC.

Strong, James. (2009). Strong's expanded exhaustive concordance of the Bible. Thomas Nelson. #H4106

Thompson, Curt. (2015). The soul of shame: Retelling the stories we believe about ourselves. IVP Books.

Townsend, John. (2011). Beyond boundaries: Learning to trust again in relationships. Zondervan.

Van der Kolk, Bessel. (2014). The body keeps the score: Brain, mind, and body in the healing of trauma. Penguin Books.

Wardle, Terry. (2005). Wounded: How to find wholeness and inner healing in Christ. Leafwood Publishers.

Woods, Ramona. (2010, June). Personal communication, coaching.

APPENDIX A

Mother Wound Assessment

Do you struggle with self-care?

Do you have challenges with female professional or personal relationships?

Do you often notice an empty feeling in the pit of your stomach?

Do you find yourself caring for others in ways you do not care for yourself?

Do you experience a high turnover rate of female staff (They last less than a year. If you don't have staff, consider other female relationships that last less than a year)?

Do you bond quickly with others only to see the bond fade and disappear?

Do you say, It's easier for me to get along with men than with women?

- - -

If you answered yes to 0–1 of the questions, it is likely this particular wound is not causing a block or barrier in your business growth. If the one question you answered yes to feels unsettled in your soul, we recommend exploring this further to experience healing in your soul.

If you answered yes to 2–3 of the questions, we encourage you to explore soul healing around this wound. Your business will likely grow, and your life will thrive as you experience more healing in this area.

If you answered yes to 4 or more of the questions, there are wounds in your soul that need to be addressed immediately. We recommend taking the brave step when you are ready to do a deep dive into how this wound is causing blocks, barriers, and blunders in your business and life.

We are waiting for you at healyourbusiness.academy and we want to take the healing journey with you.

Invitation to go Deeper

What was your relationship like with your mother?

Do you know the circumstances surrounding your birth?

Do you know your birth story?

How do you feel when you think of it?

Alignment Affirmation

I am loved. I can receive, and I can give love. I deserve to rest. I am secure in my mind, body, and soul. I don't have to do anything to earn love. I am worthy simply because I exist. My place on this earth is valuable, necessary, and irreplaceable.

APPENDIX B

Father Wound Assessment

Do you struggle to be confident in who you are?

Do you have challenges picking one business lane and saying in it?

Do you have challenges with male personal or professional relationships (lack of respect, crossing boundaries, etc.)?

Do you sense a lack of affirmation around your identity?

Do you freeze when new opportunities arise?

Do you struggle setting boundaries and maintaining them (food, work hours, relationships, etc.)?

Do you ever feel emotionally or financially insecure?

- - -

If you answered yes to 0–1 of the questions, it is likely this particular wound is not causing a block or barrier in your business growth. If the one question you answered yes to feels unsettled in your soul, we recommend exploring this further to experience healing in your soul.

If you answered yes to 2–3 of the questions, we encourage you to explore soul healing around this wound. Your business will likely grow, and your life will thrive as you experience more healing in this area.

If you answered yes to 4 or more of the questions, there are wounds in your soul that need to be addressed immediately. We recommend taking the brave step when you are ready to do a deep dive into how this wound is causing blocks, barriers, and blunders in your business and life.

We are waiting for you at healyourbusiness.academy and we want to take the healing journey with you.

Invitation to go Deeper

What was your relationship like with your father?

Was your father able to be emotionally present?

Did your father affirm your identity?

Did your father make sure the family was financially secure and spiritually grounded?

Alignment Affirmation

I am confident in my identity. I can set healthy boundaries in every aspect of my life. I am strong, secure, and I model self-control. I make good decisions, and I experience the benefits of positive decisions in my life and my business.

APPENDIX C

Wounds of Trust Assessment

Do you believe that no one can be trusted?

Do you struggle with delegating?

Do you have challenges forgiving when someone makes a mistake?

Do you find yourself keeping others at a safe distance relationally?

Do you remind yourself of reasons not to get close to those around you?

Do you feel like you're always watching and waiting for the next bad thing to happen?

Do you expect people to let you down?

Do you stay functional to avoid intimacy or closeness with others?

– – –

If you answered yes to 0–1 of the questions, it is likely this particular wound is not causing a block or barrier in your business growth. If the one question you answered yes to feels unsettled in your soul, we recommend exploring this further to experience healing in your soul.

If you answered yes to 2–3 of the questions, we encourage you to explore soul healing around this wound. Your business will likely grow, and your life will thrive as you experience more healing in this area.

If you answered yes to 4 or more of the questions, there are wounds in your soul that need to be addressed immediately. We recommend taking the brave step when you are ready to do a deep dive into how this wound is causing blocks, barriers, and blunders in your business and life.

We are waiting for you at healyourbusiness.academy and we want to take the healing journey with you.

Invitation to go Deeper

Did an adult break your trust before the age of 10?

When you consider trusting someone, do you feel anxiety in your body? Where?

Who was the first person that you remember letting you down? What happened?

Is there anyone in your life you can say you fully trust and can count on to be there for you?

Alignment Affirmation

I am not alone in this world, and others can be trusted. I am not an island. I need and desire healthy relationships where I can trust others and others can trust me. I choose to forgive anyone who has let me down or abused my trust. My wall of mistrust is demolished, and I embrace the freedom to love and experience joy.

APPENDIX D

Wounds of Abuse Assessment

Do you recall experiencing sexual abuse during your childhood by someone three years or older than you?

Do you recall experiencing physical abuse as a child?

Do you recall experiencing any form of neglect as a child (emotional, financial, medical, etc.)?

Do you consider yourself a survivor of physical, sexual, emotional, or spiritual abuse as a child or adult?

Do you sense there may be abuse in your history, but it is too difficult for you to access it or feel it?

Do you have memories of abuse that you cannot get out of your mind or body?

Do you find yourself having an intense startle reflex?

– – –

If you answered yes to any of the questions above, we encourage you to explore a soul healing journey from the wounds of abuse.

Invitation to go Deeper

What was your experience of abuse as a child?

How did the adults and caregivers around you respond to the abuse?

What is the most challenging memory or impact of the abuse for you to overcome?

Who have you shared your abuse with and allowed them to hold space for you to process? How was that experience?

Alignment Affirmation

I deserve to be protected and respected. I can set boundaries to keep me safe, I no longer live in fear, and I am not captive to past trauma. Any darkness imposed upon me cannot remain within me. Light fills my soul and shines from within me. My voice is restored, I am confident, I am worthy, and I am safe.

APPENDIX E

Wounds of Rejection Assessment

Do you recall experiencing rejection from your family of origin as a child?

Do you recall experiencing social rejection from your peers as a child (the last one picked, odd one out, etc.)?

Do you often feel like you just don't fit in with desired groups?

Do you adjust your personality, hair, values, or other traits to fit into a particular group?

Do you notice that you still feel alone or out of place when you are around people you know?

Do you experience a lump in your throat when you learn of an event or experience you wish you were included in but were not?

Do you have a list of things that if you changed, then you would be accepted more or included in desired circles of influence in your life?

Do you avoid new opportunities out of fear of failure or believe that you're not good enough for them?

- - -

If you answered yes to 0–1 of the questions, it is likely this particular wound is not causing a block or barrier in your business growth. If the one question you answered yes to feels unsettled in your soul, we recommend exploring this further to experience healing in your soul.

If you answered yes to 2–3 of the questions, we encourage you to explore soul healing around this wound. Your business will likely grow, and your life will thrive as you experience more healing in this area.

If you answered yes to 4 or more of the questions, there are wounds in your soul that need to be addressed immediately. We recommend taking the brave step when you are ready to do a deep dive into how this wound is causing blocks, barriers, and blunders in your business and life.

We are waiting for you at healyourbusiness.academy and we want to take the healing journey with you.

Invitation to go Deeper

What is your first memory of experiencing rejection?

How do you typically respond to feeling rejected?

How long do feelings of rejection linger in your heart, soul, and mind?

What does your sense of belonging feel like in your family of origin?

Alignment Affirmation

I accept and love everything about myself. I am worthy of God's best for my life, and I am approved. I am secure in who I am. I will not shrink back or hide my gifts and talents. My place in this world is necessary and validated.

APPENDIX F

Wounds of Loss Assessment

Do you recall experiencing a loss of a caregiver or a significant adult when you were a child?

Do you recall you or your family losing a house, favorite pet, or anything significant to the family when you were a child?

Do you wish you had an adult to explain the loss and help you process it when you were a child?

Have you experienced a significant relationship loss as a result of death as an adult?

Have you experienced a significant loss by choice as an adult (divorce, relocating, business closure, foreclosure, friendship, health, etc.)?

Do you find yourself needing to keep it together when you feel or think about the losses in your life?

Do you guard your heart and not get too close to others so you don't have to experience the pain of losing them?

– – –

If you answered yes to 0–1 of the questions, it is likely this particular wound is not causing a block or barrier in your business growth. If the one question you answered yes to feels unsettled in your soul, we recommend exploring this further to experience healing in your soul.

If you answered yes to 2–3 of the questions, we encourage you to explore soul healing around this wound. Your business will likely grow, and your life will thrive as you experience more healing in this area.

If you answered yes to 4 or more of the questions, there are wounds in your soul that need to be addressed immediately. We recommend taking the brave step when you are ready to do a deep dive into how this wound is causing blocks, barriers, and blunders in your business and life.

We are waiting for you at healyourbusiness.academy and we want to take the healing journey with you.

Invitation to go Deeper

What has been the greatest loss of your lifetime?

Have you allowed yourself to grieve significant losses in your life?

What do you feel in your body when you think about the loss?

How do you guard your heart against feeling the pain of things and people you've lost?

Alignment Affirmation

Everything I've lost deserves to be grieved. I can experience the pain of losing things and people I love, and it will not overtake me. There is meaning and significance in everything that has happened in my life, and although I've experienced loss, I am not lost. I am present in the here and now, I am whole, and I have everything I need.

APPENDIX G

Wounds of Unresolved Issues Assessment

Do you notice you often feel stuck in business or in life?

Do you randomly have feelings of lethargy or low motivation?

Do you know there are areas in your life that need soul healing attention?

Do you sense you should be further along in business or in life?

Do you find yourself feeling envy toward those who seem to have it together?

Do you feel people around you (past or present) have negatively contributed to your current business conditions?

Do you find yourself wishing you could just get over it or move forward even if you don't know what you're getting over, you just desire to move forward?

– – –

If you answered yes to 0–1 of the questions, it is likely this particular wound is not causing a block or barrier in your business growth. If the one question you answered yes to feels unsettled in your soul, we recommend exploring this further to experience healing in your soul.

If you answered yes to 2–3 of the questions, we encourage you to explore soul healing around this wound. Your business will likely grow, and your life will thrive as you experience more healing in this area.

If you answered yes to 4 or more of the questions, there are wounds in your soul that need to be addressed immediately. We recommend taking the brave step when you are ready to do a deep dive into how this wound is causing blocks, barriers, and blunders in your business and life.

We are waiting for you at healyourbusiness.academy and we want to take the healing journey with you.

Invitation to go Deeper

Which situations or experiences continue to cause unrest and interruptions in your life when they come up?

Which of the wounds discussed in this work has been the most significant barrier to growing your business the way you desire?

What work have you done to process wounds and trauma in your life?

What are other wounds or significant traumas in your life not addressed in this work?

Alignment Affirmation

I am free from the residual impact of wounds and trauma in my life. My experiences do not define me, and I deserve to heal completely. I permit myself to continue a healing journey, and I am healing deeper and deeper every day in every way. I am committed to Heal My Soul Heal My Business.